WRITE 10K in a DAY
Accompaniment Text

WRITING TOOLS FOR AUTHORS

Award Winning Author

LYDIA MICHAELS

WORKBOOK

Part of the Write 10K in a Day Series

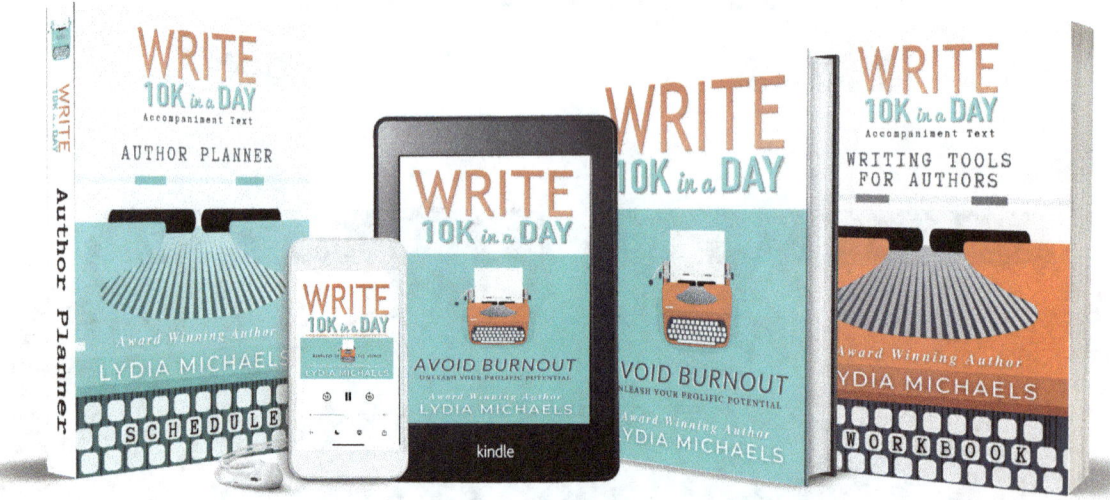

Write 10k in a Day Workbook
Written and Produced by Lydia Michaels

www.LydiaMichaelsBooks.com
© Lydia Michaels Books 2021

Published by Bailey Brown Publishing
Cover Design by Lydia Michaels
Edited by Theresa Kohler, Oxford Comma Editing

All rights reserved.
No part of this book may be reproduced in any form or by any electronic or mechanical means, including information storage and retrieval systems, without written permission from the author, except for the use of brief quotations in a book review.

TABLE OF CONTENTS

Avoid Burnout & Unleash Your Prolific Potential

5 INTRO
The Full Experience
How to Use this Workbook
Forming a Mastermind Group
Discussion Questions

THE HEALTH & WELLNESS OF A WRITER

11 CHAPTER 1: BURNOUT
QUIZ: Are You Burned Out?
Discussion Questions

6 CHAPTER 2: WAKE UP CALL
The Author Soul
Why are You an Author?

2 CHAPTER 3: A HEALTHY ROAD TO SUCCESS
Discussion Questions
Reviewing the Job

6 CHAPTER 4: STRESS
21 Days Builds a Habit
Discussion Questions

0 CHAPTER 5: DETOX
Detox Guide
Monthly Reflection

6 CHAPTER 6: BALANCE
Identify Your #1 Objective
Discussion Questions

39 CHAPTER 7: MIND OVER MATTER
Mindful Meditation Guide

41 CHAPTER 8: PUTTING A PLAN INTO MOTION
Plan for Motion

THE BUSINESS OF WRITING

44 CHAPTER 9: THE COMPANY WE KEEP
Your Mission Statement
Profit & Loss Statement
Discussion Questions
Healthy Work Habits

54 CHAPTER 10: PRODUCTIVITY
Setting Measurable Goals
What's Your Creative Process?

57 CHAPTER 11: TIME
Time Audit
One Hour Intervals
Discussion Questions

64 CHAPTER 12: SCHEDULING
Batch Your Day

67 CHAPTER 13: THE SOCIAL AUTHOR
Automate Your Life
Hashtags

www.LydiaMichaelsBooks.com

TABLE OF CONTENTS

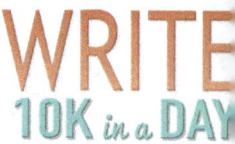

Avoid Burnout & Unleash Your Prolific Potential

70 CHAPTER 14: SOCIAL MONETIZATION
Discussion Questions
Brand Identity
Who is Your Audience?
Who is Your Target?

75 CHAPTER 15: THE PUBLISHING INDUSTRY
Constructing Query Letters
Query Tracker

83 CHAPTER 16: THE CREATIVE PROCESS
Committing to a Deadline

85 CHAPTER 17: TRANSPORTING THE READER
The Hook
Characterization Web
Character Dossier
Goal-Motivation-Conflict
Layering Suspense
Plot Waves
Book Bible Mapping
Book Bible Family Trees
Book Bible Timelines

103 CHAPTER 18: PLOT
Get Your Acts Together
The Fiction Formula
The Write 10K in a Day Outline

136 CHAPTER 19: THE ART OF WRITING
Reverse Immersion Checklist

138 CHAPTER 20: THE JOB OF EDITING
Common Typos Checklist
Deep Point of View Checklist
Discussion Questions

142 CHAPTER 21: THE TAKEAWAY
Discussion Questions

Get the Full Experience
About the Author
Books by Lydia Michaels
Notes

INTRO

"You got this."

LYDIA MICHAELS, WRITE 10K IN A DAY, 2021

WANT THE FULL EXPERIENCE?

The **Write 10K in a Day Workbook** is part of the *Write 10K in a Day* series which includes Lydia Michaels's groundbreaking author guide, **Write 10K in a Day: Avoid Burnout and Unleash Your Prolific Potential** (available in print, digital, and **audiobook**), and the **Write 10K in a Day Author Planner**. Each chapter of the **Write 10K in a Day Workbook** coordinates with the **Write 10K in a Day** primary text.

Write 10K in a Day takes a comprehensive look at finding a healthy balance between life and time on the job, business essentials such as the publishing process, managing social media, and achieving sustainable success in the book industry. Michaels shares years of experience in a warm and personal manner that grips the reader, inspires, and even gets a few laughs.

For educational videos, author resources, and ongoing inspiration, follow Lydia Michaels and the *Write 10K in a Day* series on Instagram **@Write10KinaDay** and **@Lydia_Michaels_Books**.

Do you have suggestions to improve this workbook or other books in the Write 10K in a Day series?

Email Lydia Michaels at Lydia@LydiaMichaelsBooks.com.

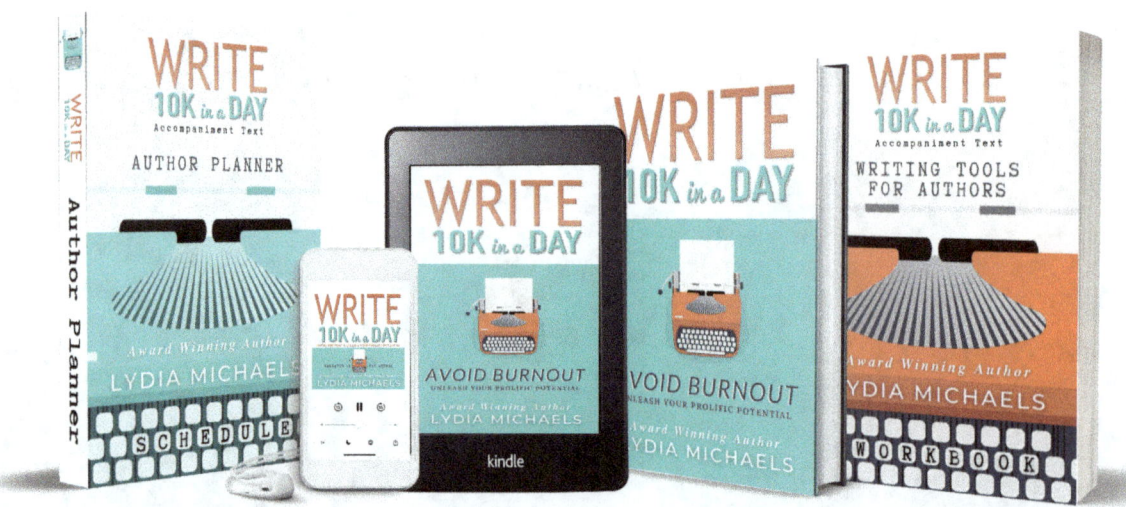

HOW TO USE THIS WORKBOOK

The **Write 10K in a Day Workbook** is an accompaniment text to the groundbreaking author guide, **Write 10K in a Day: Avoid Burnout and Unleash Your Prolific Potential** (available in print, digital, and audiobook).

The resources in this workbook are linked to the *Write 10K in a Day* series. When authors use the series as a set, they have a more comprehensive understanding of the methodology and why certain exercises are particularly helpful to author success.

The chapters ahead are based on chapters of the *Write 10K in a Day* primary text, featuring activities and discussion questions to help authors avoid burnout and unleash their prolific potential.

To take an active approach with the *Write 10K in a Day* philosophies and make the most out of the experience, please consider the following tips.

TIPS TO GET STARTED

- Read **Write 10K in a Day**
- Form a **Mastermind Group** with Authors if you prefer working with peers
- Review the **Discussion Questions** independently or with your mastermind group
- Start managing your energy and avoid wasting time by using the **Write 10K in a Day Author Planner**
- Complete the activities in the **Write 10K in a Day Workbook** to streamline your creative process and direct your path to sustainable success
- Follow Write 10K in a Day and Lydia Michaels on **Instagram** to stay informed about strategies and tools @Write10KinaDay @Lydia_Michaels_Books

www.LydiaMichaelsBooks.com

FORMING A MASTERMIND GROUP

Now that you've begun reading *Write 10K in a Day*, you will want to form a mastermind group of like-minded professionals who share similar goals for success. If you are unsure where to find such people, try posting on social media or reaching out in the **Instagram** comment section **@Write10KinaDay**. We love to help authors connect and network in the writing community!

Although some lessons can be more beneficial when reviewed as a group, this workbook can be just as valuable to authors who prefer to work independently and take the needed time for self-reflection.

TIPS TO FORM A MASTERMIND GROUP:

1. Identify and clearly define the areas of focus for your mastermind group
2. Determine how many members you will allow to join your group
3. Set basic rules for the group
4. Define the group's policies for members
5. Outline the structure of meetings. Will there be guest speakers? How formal will the meetings be?
6. How often will the group meet? Will there be weekly, monthly, quarterly, or annual meetings? Or will communication between members occur more casually on a random, perhaps virtual, platform?
7. Determine where the group will meet. Is this a virtual group or a physical group? Some location options include: a hotel boardroom, cafe, public library, community center, in a home, bar, restaurant, and so on.
8. Will there be a membership fee? Will there be recurring dues? What will membership cost? What expenses will be covered?

"Being an author is an isolated profession, but it does not have to be a lonely one. Your people are out there. Take a leadership role, form a mastermind group of your own, and find them."

Lydia Michaels, Write 10K in a Day, 2021

MASTERMIND GROUP

GROUP NAME

GROUP SIZE

MEMBER TRAITS

GROUP CREATOR

FOUNDING MEMBERS

SNAPSHOT OF GROUP

Objective	Frequency	Structure

BUDGET OVERVIEW

Guest Speakers	Location	Membership Dues

RULES & POLICIES

THE HEALTH *part one* AND WELLNESS OF A WRITER

WRITE 10K in a DAY

www.LydiaMichaelsBooks.com

CHAPTER ONE
BURNOUT

"*A good novel tells us the truth about its hero; but a bad novel tells us the truth about its author.*"

G.K. CHESTERTON, HERETICS, 1905

ARE YOU SUFFERING BURNOUT

RATE YOURSELF ON THE FOLLOWING QUESTIONS. ONCE COMPLETE, ADD UP YOUR SCORE

WRITE 10K in a DAY

	Strongly Disagree	Mostly Disagree	Equally Agree & Disagree	Mostly Agree	Strongly Agree
MOST DAYS, I'M DRAINED OF PHYSICAL OR EMOTIONAL ENERGY	1	2	3	4	5
I HAVE HAD NEGATIVE AND CYNICAL FEELINGS ABOUT WORK LATELY	1	2	3	4	5
I AM IMPATIENT WITH OTHERS	1	2	3	4	5
I AM UNSATISFIED WITH THE JOB I'M DOING AND RESULTS I'M GETTING	1	2	3	4	5
I AM EASILY FRUSTRATED BY COMPLICATIONS OR OTHERS IN MY LINE OF WORK	1	2	3	4	5
NO ONE IN MY LIFE UNDERSTANDS MY JOB OR HOW DIFFICULT IT IS	1	2	3	4	5
I SOMETIMES CONSIDER CHANGING PROFESSIONS	1	2	3	4	5
I FEEL MY EFFORT AT WORK IS UNDERAPPRECIATED	1	2	3	4	5
I FEEL EXTREME PRESSURE TO ACCOMPLISH MORE	1	2	3	4	5
INDUSTRY AND/OR PLATFORM POLICIES AND PRACTICES OFTEN HINDER MY SUCCESS	1	2	3	4	5
I AM NOT AS SUCCESSFUL AS I SHOULD BE	1	2	3	4	5
LATELY, I SUFFER FROM BRAIN FOG	1	2	3	4	5
THERE IS NOT ENOUGH TIME IN THE DAY TO ACCOMPLISH ALL THAT NEEDS TO BE DONE	1	2	3	4	5
TOO MANY TASKS REQUIRE MY ATTENTION, THEREFORE I CANNOT GIVE 100% OF MY FOCUS TO ANYTHING	1	2	3	4	5
I TEND TO PROCRASTINATE AT WORK MORE THAN USUAL	1	2	3	4	5

TOTAL: ___ + ___ + ___ + ___ + ___ = ___

ARE YOU SUFFERING BURNOUT?

NOW, COMPARE YOUR RESULTS TO THE CHART BELOW. MORE INFORMATION ABOUT BURNOUT AND WAYS TO RECOVER FROM BURNOUT CAN BE FOUND IN WRITE 10K IN A DAY.

What does your score say about you?

Score	
65-75 **BURNED-OUT**	You are burned-out and in need of break. Chances are, you're feeling unappreciated and in need of some incentives on the job. Right now, you are too overworked and overstressed to make any life-altering decisions, so put work on hold and take some time to regroup. As your stress diminishes, so should any physical symptoms such as stress related health issues and fatigue.
50-64 **BURNING OUT**	You are likely suffering early symptoms of burnout such as headaches, changes in sleep habits, avoiding work, and/or a negative mindset. It's time for a break to recharge. Take time to prioritize your world. Consider why you became an author and what you want to get out of the job and your life.
39-49 **CAUTION NEEDED**	Some days you're in your groove, but other days you feel like giving up. You teeter on the cusp of burnout, which is a dangerous place to live. It's recommended that you work on replacing bad habits with better ones and take an audit of how you're spending time. Try to identify the trigger of those bad days and replace it with a proactive tool that helps you work more efficiently.
30-38 **CONTROLLED**	Keep an eye open for any particularly high scores, as they could become triggers for future burnout. Without any extremely high areas, it appears you have control over the job and balance between life and work. Treat yourself to something nice the next time you accomplish a goal.
20-29 **BALANCED**	If you have one severely polarized response, it will need attention. Otherwise, you seem to have a decent handle on a job that is both challenging and fulfilling at this time, and you're living a balanced life.
15-20 **ZEN**	Totally zen! Great job and keep up the good work. It appears that you are in a balanced state and meeting your needs at work.

DISCUSSION QUESTIONS

CHAPTER ONE
BURNOUT

Have you ever experienced burnout? Are you currently battling symptoms or consequences of burnout? If so, which ones?

YOUR ANSWER

QUESTIONS & THOUGHTS

GROUP DISCUSSION NOTES

DISCUSSION QUESTIONS

CHAPTER ONE
BURNOUT

Do you feel in control of your success? Do you question the value of certain business practices? If so, which ones? Which practices do you wish you could avoid and why?

YOUR ANSWER

QUESTIONS & THOUGHTS

GROUP DISCUSSION NOTES

CHAPTER TWO
WAKE UP CALL

"Like a gulp of wine late in the afternoon, it makes you shudder. My feet tingle. I thought I was going to die the very next moment. But I didn't die..."

JACK KEROUAC, THE DHARMA BUMS, 1959

MIND, BODY, & SPIRIT
THE AUTHOR SOUL

The physical, emotional, and creative health of the author relies on the connectivity between the mind, body, and spirit, collectively referred to as the "author soul." The author soul must be **balanced** and grounded in *awareness* to obtain long-term, sustainable success. Without a balanced author soul, symptoms of burnout will appear.

Authors cannot focus on the business and creativity (mind and spirit) alone. The body is the author's vehicle, and a healthy body is the key to creative success.

(The following activity will help you determine **WHY** you are an author.)

"Taking care of you, mentally, physically, and spiritually, is the first step in your journey to success."

Lydia Michaels, Write 10K in a Day, 2021

A WELL-ROUNDED AUTHOR SOUL PROMOTES AUTHOR SUCCESS.

www.LydiaMichaelsBooks.com

WHY ARE YOU AN AUTHOR?

Find a quiet place away from distractions, silence all notifications, and set a 10 minute timer. Use the provided space to practice **stream of consciousness writing**, with the single intention of answering the following question:

WHAT DO YOU WANT TO GAIN FROM A CAREER AS AN AUTHOR?

TO BEGIN stream of consciousness writing, simply start writing. Try to write continuously for ten minutes, and do not stop until time runs out. Waste no time on grammar or spelling. The thoughts that land on the page(s) should be uninterrupted, unedited, and unstructured.

When you're finished, your words should reveal quite a bit about your goals.

EXAMPLE:

Writing books. Peaceful. Cathartic. Let go. Characters. Falling in love. Joy. Thinking. Clarity. Ease. State of mind. Inspiration. Peace. Hope. Relatability. Inspiring others. Happiness. Balanced. Independence. Human connection. Making a living. A sense of pride. The absolute joy of writing. Challenging myself...

WHAT DO YOU WANT TO GAIN FROM A CAREER AS AN AUTHOR?

WHAT DO YOU WANT TO GAIN FROM A CAREER AS AN AUTHOR?

WHAT DO YOU WANT TO GAIN FROM A CAREER AS AN AUTHOR?

CHAPTER THREE
A HEALTHY ROAD TO SUCCESS

"Every human being is the author of his own health or disease."

SWAMI SIVANANDA, BLISS DIVINE, 1974

DISCUSSION QUESTIONS
CHAPTER THREE
A HEALTHY ROAD TO SUCCESS

What is your current word count average? How frequently do you write? How long does it take you to write a novel from start to finish? Does this include time spent editing and polishing the project? How would you like to see your time improve?

YOUR ANSWER

QUESTIONS & THOUGHTS

GROUP DISCUSSION NOTES

DISCUSSION QUESTIONS

CHAPTER THREE
A HEALTHY ROAD TO SUCCESS

What setbacks are preventing you from writing as often as you would like? Is there a way you could delegate "outside responsibilities" to make more time for writing? Are there any "time wasting" activities you could give up? How can you improve your situation?

YOUR ANSWER

QUESTIONS & THOUGHTS

GROUP DISCUSSION NOTES

REVIEWING THE JOB

Fill in the sections below to assess your current feelings on being an "author" versus being a "writer". Then decide what your objective is to better determine what behaviors you can change.

What I love about being a writer:	What I dislike about being an author:

My Objective is:

_____
_____
_____
_____
_____
_____

Revealing your #1 Objective takes a great deal of reflection and can prove incredibly beneficial to the direction of your career. This topic is addressed in great length in Write 10K in a Day.

www.LydiaMichaelsBooks.com

CHAPTER FOUR STRESS

"Had I died, it would have been self-destruction."

JANE AUSTEN, SENSE AND SENSIBILITY, 1811

21 DAYS BUILDS A HABIT

USE THE CHART ON THE FOLLOWING PAGE TO TRACK YOUR PROGRESS AND BUILD CONSISTENCY INTO YOUR DAILY ROUTINE.

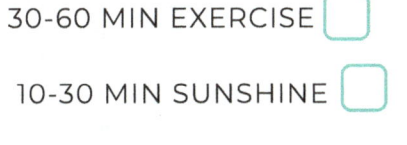

Twenty-one days can build a habit. How can your life improve in less than one month? Use the following chart objectives to monitor your daily sun exposure, exercise, nutrition, water intake, self-care, and sleep. Set a goal to meet each objective every day. Mark off each accomplished objective and watch your daily routine improve for the better when you focus on consistency!

The six simple objectives of this activity have all been linked to **boosting the immune system**. A strong immune system is key to avoiding burnout and unleashing an author's prolific potential.

BOOST YOUR IMMUNE SYSTEM

www.LydiaMichaelsBooks.com

21 DAYS BUILDS A HABIT
TWENTY-ONE

WRITE 10K IN A DAY

DAY 1
- 6-8 HRS SLEEP ☐
- 5 SERVINGS FRUITS & VEGGIES 🍎🍎🍎🍎🍎
- 30 MIN REST & SELF-CARE ☐
- 30-60 MIN EXERCISE ☐
- 10-30 MIN SUNSHINE ☐
- 8 X 8 OZ WATER 💧💧💧💧💧💧💧💧

DAY 2
- 6-8 HRS SLEEP ☐
- 5 SERVINGS FRUITS & VEGGIES 🍎🍎🍎🍎🍎
- 30 MIN REST & SELF-CARE ☐
- 30-60 MIN EXERCISE ☐
- 10-30 MIN SUNSHINE ☐
- 8 X 8 OZ WATER 💧💧💧💧💧💧💧💧

DAY 3
- 6-8 HRS SLEEP ☐
- 5 SERVINGS FRUITS & VEGGIES 🍎🍎🍎🍎🍎
- 30 MIN REST & SELF-CARE ☐
- 30-60 MIN EXERCISE ☐
- 10-30 MIN SUNSHINE ☐
- 8 X 8 OZ WATER 💧💧💧💧💧💧💧💧

DAY 4
- 6-8 HRS SLEEP ☐
- 5 SERVINGS FRUITS & VEGGIES 🍎🍎🍎🍎🍎
- 30 MIN REST & SELF-CARE ☐
- 30-60 MIN EXERCISE ☐
- 10-30 MIN SUNSHINE ☐
- 8 X 8 OZ WATER 💧💧💧💧💧💧💧💧

DAY 5
- 6-8 HRS SLEEP ☐
- 5 SERVINGS FRUITS & VEGGIES 🍎🍎🍎🍎🍎
- 30 MIN REST & SELF-CARE ☐
- 30-60 MIN EXERCISE ☐
- 10-30 MIN SUNSHINE ☐
- 8 X 8 OZ WATER 💧💧💧💧💧💧💧💧

DAY 6
- 6-8 HRS SLEEP ☐
- 5 SERVINGS FRUITS & VEGGIES 🍎🍎🍎🍎🍎
- 30 MIN REST & SELF-CARE ☐
- 30-60 MIN EXERCISE ☐
- 10-30 MIN SUNSHINE ☐
- 8 X 8 OZ WATER 💧💧💧💧💧💧💧💧

DAY 7
- 6-8 HRS SLEEP ☐
- 5 SERVINGS FRUITS & VEGGIES 🍎🍎🍎🍎🍎
- 30 MIN REST & SELF-CARE ☐
- 30-60 MIN EXERCISE ☐
- 10-30 MIN SUNSHINE ☐
- 8 X 8 OZ WATER 💧💧💧💧💧💧💧💧

DAY 8
- 6-8 HRS SLEEP ☐
- 5 SERVINGS FRUITS & VEGGIES 🍎🍎🍎🍎🍎
- 30 MIN REST & SELF-CARE ☐
- 30-60 MIN EXERCISE ☐
- 10-30 MIN SUNSHINE ☐
- 8 X 8 OZ WATER 💧💧💧💧💧💧💧💧

DAY 9
- 6-8 HRS SLEEP ☐
- 5 SERVINGS FRUITS & VEGGIES 🍎🍎🍎🍎🍎
- 30 MIN REST & SELF-CARE ☐
- 30-60 MIN EXERCISE ☐
- 10-30 MIN SUNSHINE ☐
- 8 X 8 OZ WATER 💧💧💧💧💧💧💧💧

DAY 10
- 6-8 HRS SLEEP ☐
- 5 SERVINGS FRUITS & VEGGIES 🍎🍎🍎🍎🍎
- 30 MIN REST & SELF-CARE ☐
- 30-60 MIN EXERCISE ☐
- 10-30 MIN SUNSHINE ☐
- 8 X 8 OZ WATER 💧💧💧💧💧💧💧💧

DAY 11
- 6-8 HRS SLEEP ☐
- 5 SERVINGS FRUITS & VEGGIES 🍎🍎🍎🍎🍎
- 30 MIN REST & SELF-CARE ☐
- 30-60 MIN EXERCISE ☐
- 10-30 MIN SUNSHINE ☐
- 8 X 8 OZ WATER 💧💧💧💧💧💧💧💧

DAY 12
- 6-8 HRS SLEEP ☐
- 5 SERVINGS FRUITS & VEGGIES 🍎🍎🍎🍎🍎
- 30 MIN REST & SELF-CARE ☐
- 30-60 MIN EXERCISE ☐
- 10-30 MIN SUNSHINE ☐
- 8 X 8 OZ WATER 💧💧💧💧💧💧💧💧

DAY 13
- 6-8 HRS SLEEP ☐
- 5 SERVINGS FRUITS & VEGGIES 🍎🍎🍎🍎🍎
- 30 MIN REST & SELF-CARE ☐
- 30-60 MIN EXERCISE ☐
- 10-30 MIN SUNSHINE ☐
- 8 X 8 OZ WATER 💧💧💧💧💧💧💧💧

DAY 14
- 6-8 HRS SLEEP ☐
- 5 SERVINGS FRUITS & VEGGIES 🍎🍎🍎🍎🍎
- 30 MIN REST & SELF-CARE ☐
- 30-60 MIN EXERCISE ☐
- 10-30 MIN SUNSHINE ☐
- 8 X 8 OZ WATER 💧💧💧💧💧💧💧💧

DAY 15
- 6-8 HRS SLEEP ☐
- 5 SERVINGS FRUITS & VEGGIES 🍎🍎🍎🍎🍎
- 30 MIN REST & SELF-CARE ☐
- 30-60 MIN EXERCISE ☐
- 10-30 MIN SUNSHINE ☐
- 8 X 8 OZ WATER 💧💧💧💧💧💧💧💧

DAY 16
- 6-8 HRS SLEEP ☐
- 5 SERVINGS FRUITS & VEGGIES 🍎🍎🍎🍎🍎
- 30 MIN REST & SELF-CARE ☐
- 30-60 MIN EXERCISE ☐
- 10-30 MIN SUNSHINE ☐
- 8 X 8 OZ WATER 💧💧💧💧💧💧💧💧

DAY 17
- 6-8 HRS SLEEP ☐
- 5 SERVINGS FRUITS & VEGGIES 🍎🍎🍎🍎🍎
- 30 MIN REST & SELF-CARE ☐
- 30-60 MIN EXERCISE ☐
- 10-30 MIN SUNSHINE ☐
- 8 X 8 OZ WATER 💧💧💧💧💧💧💧💧

DAY 18
- 6-8 HRS SLEEP ☐
- 5 SERVINGS FRUITS & VEGGIES 🍎🍎🍎🍎🍎
- 30 MIN REST & SELF-CARE ☐
- 30-60 MIN EXERCISE ☐
- 10-30 MIN SUNSHINE ☐
- 8 X 8 OZ WATER 💧💧💧💧💧💧💧💧

DAY 19
- 6-8 HRS SLEEP ☐
- 5 SERVINGS FRUITS & VEGGIES 🍎🍎🍎🍎🍎
- 30 MIN REST & SELF-CARE ☐
- 30-60 MIN EXERCISE ☐
- 10-30 MIN SUNSHINE ☐
- 8 X 8 OZ WATER 💧💧💧💧💧💧💧💧

DAY 20
- 6-8 HRS SLEEP ☐
- 5 SERVINGS FRUITS & VEGGIES 🍎🍎🍎🍎🍎
- 30 MIN REST & SELF-CARE ☐
- 30-60 MIN EXERCISE ☐
- 10-30 MIN SUNSHINE ☐
- 8 X 8 OZ WATER 💧💧💧💧💧💧💧💧

DAY 21
- 6-8 HRS SLEEP ☐
- 5 SERVINGS FRUITS & VEGGIES 🍎🍎🍎🍎🍎
- 30 MIN REST & SELF-CARE ☐
- 30-60 MIN EXERCISE ☐
- 10-30 MIN SUNSHINE ☐
- 8 X 8 OZ WATER 💧💧💧💧💧💧💧💧

DISCUSSION QUESTIONS

CHAPTER FOUR
STRESS

Have you suffered the Let-Down effect as an author? What high stress events contributed to slowing your overall efficiency? How could you prevent this repeat response in the future?

YOUR ANSWER

QUESTIONS & THOUGHTS

GROUP DISCUSSION NOTES

CHAPTER FIVE DETOX

> *"We all know that words have an enormous influence on the way we think and feel, and that things generally go more smoothly when positive words are used."*
>
> MASARU EMOTO, THE HIDDEN MESSAGES IN WATER, 1999

A GUIDE TO DETOXIFYING YOUR LIFE

> *"Positivity manifests positive outcomes. Negativity attracts failure and toxicity."*
> Lydia Michaels, Write 10K in a Day, 2021

The goal is progress! Think of detoxification as a part of your ever-improving journey as a well-balanced human being and author. Detoxing your life on a regular basis will keep things operating smoothly.

PRE-DETOX STEPS

1. Meditate. Visualize yourself living in a less cluttered, less toxic environment. This includes physical, mental, digital, spiritual, and emotional clutter, so evaluate all the baggage you're packing on this journey. It's time to get rid of anything holding you down. Picture yourself enjoying a balanced mind and healthy body. What does that look like? Try to picture all the qualities of such a life. Imagine how a less cluttered life will feed your creative spirit.

2. Establish a healthy reward system. Practice pausing after activities that are mentally or physically strenuous to appreciate what you just accomplished. Practice this method of mindfulness and gratitude often. If you struggle to celebrate accomplishments, consider starting a gratitude journal.

WHAT ARE THE QUALITIES OF A BALANCED LIFE?

_____
_____
_____
_____
_____
_____
_____
_____

LIST 10 THINGS YOU'RE GRATEFUL FOR

_____
_____
_____
_____
_____
_____
_____

www.LydiaMichaelsBooks.com

DETOXIFYING YOUR LIFE

3. Reestablish a healthy sleep schedule designed to maintain 6-8 hours of sleep a night. If needed, use technology to set alerts for waking and winding down. Research shows poor sleep habits can have a negative effect on brain function and health. For the best sleep environment, minimize external noise and both artificial and natural light.

WHAT TIME SHOULD YOU WAKE UP? _____

WHAT TIME SHOULD YOU FALL ASLEEP TO ALLOW 8 FULL HOURS OF SLEEP? _____

HOW MUCH DOWN TIME WILL YOU NEED BEFORE SLEEP? _____

WHAT TIME SHOULD YOU GO TO BED TO ALLOW FOR DOWN TIME? _____

4. If you are not drinking the daily recommended amount of water, start meeting the suggested 8 ounce glasses of water 8 times a day. This will begin the process of physically flushing toxins from your system. Water is so important to the body's healing process, and so many people undervalue its benefits.

- If staying hydrated is a challenge for you, try using a 32 oz. water bottle and drinking its contents 3-4 times a day.
- Use an 8 oz water bottle and keep 8 rubber bands on the bottle. Every time you refill the bottle, move a rubber band to your wrist. The goal is to have all 8 rubber bands on your wrist by the end of the day.
- Set a soft timer on your phone to chime every 30 minutes throughout the day as a reminder to sip some water.

HOW WILL YOU DETOX YOUR LIFE?

1. Detox your physical environment. This requires you to clean your office, home, and car. The objective is not to polish the furniture but declutter. Every item you own should have a home. Dispose of or donate any unwanted items.

WHAT PHYSICAL SPACES IN YOUR LIFE NEED ORGANIZATION?

_____
_____
_____
_____
_____
_____
_____

2. Detox functional spaces. For some, this might mean organizing a cosmetic area or shoe rack. For others, it might be a tool shed or silverware drawer. The idea is to hit each closet, compartment, and/or garage until order is restored. Think functionality over vanity.

WHAT SMALL, FUNCTIONAL SPACES IN YOUR LIFE COULD FUNCTION BETTER IF DECLUTTERED?

_____
_____
_____
_____
_____
_____
_____

3. Detox your digital devices. Organize your computer files, remove any apps you don't use from your computer or phone, empty your inbox and set filters by unsubscribing from mailing lists you steadily ignore, run all updates, cancel unwanted subscriptions, especially those forgettable ones that bill on a cycle, and evaluate your notification settings.

WHAT DIGITAL AREAS OF YOUR LIFE NEED ORGANIZATION?
_____
_____
_____
_____

4. Detox your relationships. Start with an overhaul of your virtual friends. Without getting lost in social media, focus only on your follower/friends lists. Next, declutter the list of people you are following. Stop following people who only make you feel bad about yourself! Then move on to your real-life relationships and appraise each one realistically. If someone in your life does not inspire positive emotions, ask yourself if you share a healthy relationship. Cut away the dead relationships, say goodbye to the toxic people in your life, those who only stir negative thoughts and feelings. And for the toxic relationships you can't totally cut off, establish boundaries. Maintain a healthy distance and revisit the relationship again in the future. Ideally, the people in your life should inspire and motivate you. They should lift you up and fill you with light. Life is too short to waste time on toxic relationships or toxic people.

WRITE A MEMORABLE STATEMENT OR QUESTION TO MONITOR THE HEALTH OF YOUR RELATIONSHIPS.
(Example: Does this person bring inspiration, motivation, education, or joy to my life? Do they create negative emotions?)
_____
_____
_____

5. Detox your mind. Meditate and pay special attention to the airiness where sludge might have existed before. Your state of mind should feel less overwhelming after accomplishing the prior steps. Express gratitude for this rediscovered openness. Recognize that you are a masterpiece in the making. With patience and balance anything is possible.

WRITE AN AFFIRMATION THAT IS IN LINE WITH YOUR NEW PERSPECTIVE:

_____

6. Detox your routine. As you prepare to change your life, do not rush back into the toxic patterns you ran from before. Now is the time to simplify your routine. Take time to plan it. *(More tips on scheduling ahead!)*

WHAT DOES YOUR IDEAL DAY LOOK LIKE?

TIME	SCHEDULE

CHAPTER SIX
BALANCE

"*'Here's a nice image for a life in balance,' she said. 'You're juggling these four balls that you've named work, family, friends, spirit. Now, work is a rubber ball. If you drop it, it bounces back. The other balls they're made of glass.'*

'I've dropped a few of those glass balls in my day. Sometimes they chip, sometimes they shatter to pieces.'"

JAMES PATTERSON, ROSES ARE RED, 2001

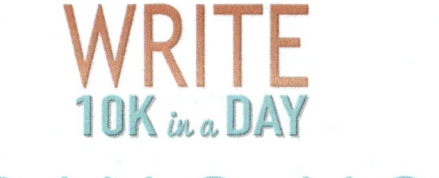

FINDING YOUR
#1 OBJECTIVE

"Your #1 Objective is your greatest goal in life. It's an ultimate priority used to navigate the path to professional and personal success."

Lydia Michaels, Write 10K in a Day, 2021

1. Go to a quiet place with few distractions.

2. Shut off all notifications so you are not disturbed.

3. Set a timer for 30 minutes.

4. Ask yourself what is it you want out of life and compile a list.

5. Simplify and prioritize your list until you narrow your objective down to one blanket term. (It's okay to do this multiple times and keep a journal of your thoughts and revelations.)

Your #1 Objective.

_____
_____
_____
_____
_____
_____
_____
_____
_____
_____
_____
_____

DISCUSSION QUESTION

CHAPTER SIX
BALANCE

How will you measure success? Define your measurement of success below.

YOUR ANSWER

QUESTIONS & THOUGHTS

GROUP DISCUSSION NOTES

CHAPTER SEVEN
MIND OVER MATTER

"*Fear comes with imagination, it's a penalty, it's the price of imagination.*"

THOMAS HARRIS, RED DRAGON, 1981

A Guide to Mindfulness Meditation

Mindfulness meditation is the practice of existing in the present moment and accepting circumstances without judgement. It is a state of relaxed awareness that can reduce stress and increase clarity, leading to a calmer, happier life.

GETTING STARTED

1. Choose a set length of time to practice mindfulness meditation each day (10-15 minutes is a great start). Consistency is key to creating good habits.
2. Disconnect from all digital notifications and distractions.
3. Choose a quiet place where you can safely clear your mind. Some prefer to sit while others prefer to walk.
4. Invite positive vibes and avoid letting thoughts turn to self-criticism.
5. Clear your mind by putting aside all "to do" thoughts. It's natural for the mind to wander. Notice the thought, pause to acknowledge it for later consideration, then come back to the present and empty the mind.
6. To detach from distractions and settle the mind, mentally scan the body, deliberately feeling all sensations from head to toe (the sounds entering the ears, the breath in your nose and lungs, the weight of your skin, the strength of your muscles, etc.) and allow gratitude that you are alive to warm your soul.
7. After you've met your commitment, return to your typical routine refreshed, less stressed, and clearheaded.
8. Keep a mindfulness journal. After meditation, jot down any pressing revelations.

"You don't have to be a monk to disconnect and practice mindfulness."

Lydia Michaels, Write 10K in a Day, 2021

CHAPTER EIGHT
PUTTING A PLAN INTO MOTION

"An early-morning walk is a blessing for the whole day."

HENRY DAVID THOREAU, WALDEN, 1854

PLANNING LEADS TO MOTION
MOTION LEADS TO BALANCE
BALANCE LEADS TO SUCCESS

GET MOTIVATED TO MOVE MORE

WRITING DOWN A PLAN CAN INCREASE YOUR CHANCES FOR SUCCESS BY 42%

HOW CAN YOU INCORPORATE MORE MOVEMENT BREAKS INTO YOUR WORKDAY?

TIPS TO INCREASE MOVEMENT

- Put sneakers on in the morning
- Set alarms for movement breaks
- Get up every hour
- Wear a pedometer
- Walk the dog
- Walk on your lunch break
- Park far away
- Pace while working
- Walk while making phone calls
- Form a daily walking group
- Keep a list of places to walk
- Listen to audiobooks
- Listen to podcasts
- Listen to workshops
- Listen to music
- A 10 min walk still counts!
- Share your journey on social apps
- Take a quick walk around the block
- Add 500 steps before bed

WHAT'S YOUR PLAN FOR MORE MOTION?

_____
_____
_____
_____
_____
_____
_____
_____
_____
_____
_____
_____
_____
_____

"Movement is an ultimate balancing tool. Walking is one of the fastest steps you can take toward correcting imbalances and recovering from burnout."

Lydia Michaels, Write 10K in a Day, 2021

THE BUSINESS
part two
OF WRITING

www.LydiaMichaelsBooks.com

CHAPTER NINE
THE COMPANY WE KEEP

"I will not follow where the path may lead, but I will go where there is no path, and I will leave a trail."

MURIEL STRODE, WIND-WAFTED WILDFLOWERS, 1903

MISSION
your company's
STATEMENT

WHO IS YOUR TARGET AUDIENCE?
_____
_____
_____

WHAT PRODUCT OR SERVICE DO YOU CONTRIBUTE TO YOUR INDUSTRY?
_____
_____
_____

WHAT MAKES YOUR PRODUCTS OR SERVICES UNIQUELY DIFFERENT FROM THE COMPETITION?
_____
_____
_____

WHY DOES YOUR COMPANY DO WHAT IT DOES?
_____
_____
_____

PUT IT ALL TOGETHER TO BUILD YOUR MISSION STATEMENT:
_____
_____
_____

The *profit and loss (P&L) statement* is a financial statement that summarizes the revenues, costs, and expenses incurred during a specified period, usually a fiscal quarter or year.

PROFIT & LOSS STATEMENT

TO MAKE A PROFIT & LOSS STATEMENT

1. List all sources of revenue and calculate each revenue on a uniform timetable (e.g. monthly or annually)

2. The sum of all revenues will be your gross profit

3. List and calculate all production costs and operating expenses using the same time measurement as above

4. Deduct the sum of all business expenses from your gross profit

(Don't forget your personal wages!)

5. This will give you the net profit of your company and tell you a lot about the overall health of your business.

P&L KEY POINTS

- P&L statements are a financial snapshot of a company's revenue during a specific period
- Companies often create a P&L quarterly and annually for tax purposes
- P&L statements show a company's financial health over time
- P&L statements allow business owners a clear picture of revenue, cash flow, profitable practices, and non grossing practices that lack a measurable return on investment

SAMPLE P&L STATEMENT
USE THIS MODEL TO CREATE YOUR OWN

WENDY WRITESALOT BOOKS, LLC

Wendy Writesalot
117 Inkwell Avenue
New York, NY 10001
WendyWritesalot.com

DATE : JANUARY 1, 2019 - DECEMBER 31, 2019
PROFIT & LOSS STATEMENT

REVENUE	SUBTOTAL	GROSS PROFIT
Manuscript Dispatch	22000 USD	**90200 USD**
PayFriend	7950 USD	
Book Depot	17200 USD	
Audio Inventory	10950 USD	
Big 6 Publishing House	32100 USD	
Total Income:	**90200 USD**	

BUSINESS EXPENSES	SUBTOTAL	TOTAL EXPENSES
Scheduling App	140 USD	**82771 USD**
Form App	280 USD	
Banking Maintenance Fees	120 USD	
Website Hosting	450 USD	NET PROFIT
Postage (S&H)	834 USD	
Marketing Services Inc.	3500 USD	**7429 USD**
Book Trailers	600 USD	
Audiobook Productions	4500 USD	
Social Media Ads	24000 USD	
Office Supplies	550 USD	
Cover Art	990 USD	
Digital Storage	240 USD	
ISBNs	300 USD	
Books (Research)	180 USD	
Book Inventory	5850 USD	
Merchandise	1200 USD	
Phone Replacement	850 USD	
Editor Services	6100 USD	
Administrative Assistant	10000 USD	
eBook Delivery Fees	1387 USD	
Print Proofs	700 USD	
Author Wages	20000 USD	
Total Business Expenses:	**82771 USD**	

OTHER EXPENSES TO CONSIDER

- Travel
- Vehicle
- Healthcare
- Home Office
  (% base on home office SF)
- Office Furniture
- Internet
- Phone Service
- Electric
- Water/Sewer
- Heat
- Parking Garage(s)
- Fuel
- Tolls
- Hotel
- Conventions
- Workshops
- Education
- Subscriptions

Speak to your accountant about possible deductions.

www.LydiaMichaelsBooks.com

DISCUSSION QUESTION

CHAPTER NINE
THE COMPANY WE KEEP

As your success grows, so will your business needs. What does your dream office look like? Use the space below to design the perfect headquarters for your company.

YOUR ANSWER

QUESTIONS & THOUGHTS

GROUP DISCUSSION NOTES

HEALTHY WORK HABITS
IMPROVE YOUR LIFE

"You avoid burnout and unleash your prolific potential through self-analysis and the adoption of customized, healthy work habits."

Lydia Michaels, Write 10K in a Day, 2021

Don't just think about the healthy habits you *should* incorporate into your life, *plan how* you *will* incorporate them.

PLAN FOR SUCCESS

• **Morning Sprint:** When will your one hour sprint take place? _____

• **Take Time to Make Time:** What planning tools would make you more accountable for your time? _____

(Check out the Write 10K in a Day Author Planner)

• **Set Work Hours and Stick to Them:** When does your work day begin and end? Which days of the week will you work as an author? _____

• **Schedule According to Task:** How will you categorize your schedule? What tasks take up the majority of your time? (Example: writing, editing, marketing, personal time, office housekeeping, etc.) List 4 categories and divide common tasks (Example: bookkeeping, inventory, ad design, outlining, research, etc.) per category.

_____ _____ _____ _____

PLAN FOR SUCCESS

- **Take Meal Breaks:** Calories convert into energy. An 8 hour workday should include 1 meal and 2 snacks or 2 meals and 1 snack. What are some simple work meals that will keep you on a nutritionally balanced plan and boost your energy at work?
  _____
  _____
  _____
  _____
  _____

- **Invest in ergonomic work equipment such as yoga balls, standing desks, cozy chairs, foot stools, etc.** How can your work environment get healthier?
  _____
  _____

- **Set Timers for movement breaks and don't ignore them!** When will you schedule your movement breaks? _____

- **Schedule Personal Time:** When are your days off? How much vacation time will you allow (or enforce)? _____

- **Meditate:** When and how will you meditate? _____
  _____

- **Walk!** What is your daily step goal? How do you plan to monitor and stay accountable for accumulating those steps? _____
  _____

PLAN FOR SUCCESS

- **Clear Away Clutter:** Use the last 30 minutes of every day to clear away clutter and prepare your workspace for the next workday. How can you improve your workspace to make your daily declutter routine easier?
___
___
___
___

- **Have a Catchall:** Do you have a basket, box, briefcase, or bag to store your "current projects?" By putting projects away, you achieve a sense of completion and establish a starting point for the next day. What's your catchall? ___
___

- **Sleep 6 to 8 hours a night.** How can you improve your sleep habits? What is your set bedtime on weekdays? What is your set waking time on weekdays?
___
___
___

- **Stay hydrated!** How can you increase your water intake?
___
___
___

- **Get fresh air in your lungs and sun on your face every day!** When will you take breaks and step outside? ___

- **Listen to your body and take time off when feeling overwhelmed.** What signals does your body give when it needs a break? ___
___

PLAN FOR SUCCESS

- **Use the Word "No":** What practices should you stop agreeing to?
  _____
  _____
  _____

- **Set Boundaries!** Which of your boundaries could be strengthened?
  _____
  _____
  _____

- **Keep it Functional:** What areas of your office could be revamped to function better?
  _____

- **Live with Mindfulness:** How can you practice gratitude, live your life with purposeful intentions, and self-awareness?
  _____
  _____
  _____

- **Have Other Interests:** What hobbies are you interested in? Can you invest 2 to 4 hours a week into a hobby? When will you schedule hobby time? _____
  _____

- **Read:** What is your personal reading goal for the next year? _____
  _____

- **Resuscitate Your Social Life:** What evening will you commit to socializing? What places such as restaurants, bars, clubs, etc. would you like to try? _____
  _____

PLAN FOR SUCCESS

- **Find Joy in Cooking:** Food can either nurture the soul or infect it. What recipes would you like to try? What markets could be fun to visit? Who would you like to have as a guest at your table?

_____
_____
_____

- **Learn from Others:** Build an effective, like-minded mastermind group. Who do you find motivating, inspiring, or informative?

_____
_____
_____
_____

- **Celebrate:** Set a short-term goal and decide how you will celebrate accomplishing that goal when the time comes.

_____
_____
_____

- **Regularly Evaluate Your Team:** Are the professionals you've been working with delivering a return on your investment (ROI)? Should anyone on your team be replaced with a more effective service provider?

_____
_____
_____

- **Limit Screen Time:** When will you set a "screen-free" time each day?

_____
_____
_____

CHAPTER TEN
PRODUCTIVITY

*"Amateurs sit and wait for inspiration,
the rest of us just get up and go to work."*

STEPHEN KING, ON WRITING: A MEMOIR OF THE CRAFT, 2000

SET MEASURABLE GOALS

WRITE 10K in a DAY

"There are many ways to measure success. It's important to take time to celebrate the small victories as much as the big ones."

Lydia Michaels, Write 10K in a Day, 2021

MY GOALS	MEASUREMENT OF SUCCESS	REWARD

TRACKING MULTIPLE MEASURABLE GOALS CAN PREVENT DISCOURAGING SYMPTOMS OF BURNOUT

"Zeroing in on only one target will only devalue all your other accomplishments. And eventually, leave you discouraged."

Lydia Michaels, Write 10K in a Day, 2021
www.LydiaMichaelsBooks.com

WHAT IS YOUR CREATIVE PROCESS?

Using a creative process checklist allows authors to set limits on production cycles and establish healthy boundaries that prevent maladaptive habits, like perfectionism or impostor syndrome, which can lead to unnecessary delays. While a more challenging project might require more editing rounds than others, having such a guide keeps writers from getting carried away. It keeps the process moving and eventually forces the creator to detach from the manuscript and make room for newer works.

YOUR CREATIVE PROCESS

_____
_____
_____
_____
_____
_____
_____
_____
_____
_____
_____
_____
_____
_____
_____
_____
_____
_____
_____
_____
_____
_____

SAMPLE CREATIVE PROCESS

1. Write
2. Proof (1st Read)
3. Developmental Edits (Editor #1)
4. Revisions & Line Edits (Author)
5. Beta Read
6. Beta Revisions (Author)
7. Cover Art (eBook, Print, Audio)
8. Write Blurb
9. Assign ISBN (eBook, Print, Audio)
10. Open Pre-Orders
11. Announce Book
12. Hire PR Company & Schedule Promotion
13. Produce Audiobook
14. Proofreader (Editor #2)
15. Revisions (Author)
16. Final Read (Author)
17. Pitch (Traditional)
18. Format
19. Submit Final Manuscript
20. Distribute Advance Reviewer Copies
21. Verify all short links are active
22. RELEASE!

"The beauty of writing is that we can continuously come back and revise."

Lydia Michaels, Write 10K in a Day, 2021

CHAPTER ELEVEN
TIME

"*Life was not to be sitting in hot amorphic leisure in my backyard idly writing or not writing, as the spirit moved me. It was, instead, running madly, in a crowded schedule, in a squirrel cage of busy people. Working, living, dancing, dreaming, talking, kissing — singing, laughing, learning. The responsibility, the awful responsibility of managing (profitably) 12 hours a day for 10 weeks is rather overwhelming when there is nothing, no one, to insert an exact routine into the large unfenced acres of time — which it is so easy to let drift by in soporific idling and luxurious relaxing.*"

SYLVIA PLATH, THE UNABRIDGED JOURNALS OF SYLVIA PLATH, 2000

TIME AUDIT

"Energy is precious. It's how we manipulate the perception of time."

Lydia Michaels, Write 10K in a Day, 2021

USE THE FOLLOWING TIME AUDIT TO ANALYZE WHERE YOUR ENERGY AND HOURS ARE GOING

STEP ONE

A. Make a list of everything your job entails on any given day. Include items like bookkeeping, even if you only do this task once a month. If it's a part of your job, put it on the list.

_____   _____   _____
_____   _____   _____
_____   _____   _____
_____   _____   _____
_____   _____   _____
_____   _____   _____
_____   _____   _____
_____   _____   _____
_____   _____   _____
_____   _____   _____

B. Assign each task a value between 1-99 in the blue column. The higher the number, the higher the significance of said task. The amount of tasks listed will vary depending on the author's responsibilities. Some authors may only have 15 tasks, while others may have 75 tasks. The more tasks an author lists the less time-on-task they will have. The total sum of all task values on the list must equal 100. No less, no more. The total must be 100, as this will show the percentage of time you hope to allocate to each task. Leave the orange column blank until STEP THREE.

TIME AUDIT

C. Write out a schedule for your *ideal workday*. This should be twenty-four hours long and show everything including personal care, family time, rest, and work. *Exclude nothing*, and indulge in the fantasy of the perfect day. Be sure to leave some time for miscellaneous activities, like that pesky bookkeeping.

1:00 AM

2:00 AM

3:00 AM

4:00 AM

5:00 AM

6:00 AM

7:00 AM

8:00 AM

9:00 AM

10:00 AM

11:00 AM

12:00 PM

1:00 PM

2:00 PM

3:00 PM

4:00 PM

5:00 PM

6:00 PM

7:00 PM

8:00 PM

9:00 PM

10:00 PM

11:00 PM

12:00 AM

D. Now, put everything from STEP ONE away. You are not allowed to look at it again until you reach STEP THREE.

STEP TWO
TIME AUDIT

A. Keep a **running record** of your day from the moment you rise to the moment you go to bed. Document every task, and mark down the time. You can track your day for several days to achieve varied results.

B. Calculate your time into minutes spent on task within one 24 hour cycle.

C. For each task, divide the total minutes by 1440 (the total minutes in a 24 hour day).

MATH TIP

To convert a decimal to a percentage, multiply the number by 100 and add a % sign.

When multiplying a decimal by 100, you are essentially sliding the decimal two places to the right.

WRITE 10K in a DAY — RUNNING RECORD

TASK	MINUTES ON TASK (Y)	MINUTES DIVIDED BY 1,440 (Y ÷ 1440 = Z)	CONVERT TO PERCENTAGE (Z x 100 = ___%)
1:00 AM			
2:00 AM			
3:00 AM			
4:00 AM			
5:00 AM			
6:00 AM			
7:00 AM			
8:00 AM			
9:00 AM			
10:00 AM			
11:00 AM			
12:00 PM			
1:00 PM			
2:00 PM			
3:00 PM			
4:00 PM			
5:00 PM			
6:00 PM			
7:00 PM			
8:00 PM			
9:00 PM			
10:00 PM			
11:00 PM			
12:00 AM			

TIME AUDIT

STEP THREE

A. Return to the job list you created in **STEP ONE**. Write your actual time on task percentages from **STEP TWO** into the orange column of said task on **STEP ONE**. How does your actual percentage of time on task compare to the ideal percentage?

Perhaps you believed in STEP ONE that writing should account for at least 80% of your job, but in actuality, you're only giving it 10% of your time.

B. Where are the most major discrepancies? Where are obvious chunks of wasted time? Highlight anything that can be removed from your schedule.

_____
_____
_____
_____
_____
_____

C. Without borrowing from the time needed to sleep, do you see time spent on less crucial tasks that can be better spent on important tasks? How will you change your schedule after reviewing this data?

_____
_____
_____
_____
_____
_____
_____
_____
_____

ONE HOUR INTERVALS

"By not taking movement breaks, we are putting our health at great risk and creating negative, long-term productivity issues and inviting symptoms of burnout into our lives."

Lydia Michaels, Write 10K in a Day, 2021

EXPERIMENT

SPEND A DAY OR WEEK USING THE ONE HOUR INTERVAL TECHNIQUE.

SET A TIMER FOR ONE HOUR OR LESS. WHEN YOU ARE ALERTED BY THE TIMER, GET UP AND MOVE FOR 10-30 MINUTES.

THE BREAK MUST BE A BREAK, UNRELATED TO WORK AND YOU MAY NOT SIT DOWN.

SET A TIMER DURING YOUR BREAK, IF NEEDED, AS A REMINDER OF WHEN IT'S TIME TO GET BACK TO WORK.

THIS TIMED FOCUS STRATEGY CAN IMPROVE PRODUCTIVITY.

DISCUSSION QUESTIONS

CHAPTER ELEVEN
TIME

After conducting the one hour interval experiment, did you find yourself making better use of time on task? Did you do the experiment for one day or one week? Were you more productive? Did you accomplish more or less at the end of the day/week? Did you feel physically, mentally, or emotionally different after the experiment?

YOUR ANSWER

QUESTIONS & THOUGHTS

GROUP DISCUSSION NOTES

CHAPTER TWELVE
SCHEDULING

"A schedule defends from chaos and whim. It is a net for catching days. It is a scaffolding on which a worker can stand and labor with both hands at sections of time."

ANNIE DILLARD, THE WRITING LIFE, 1989

BATCH YOUR DAY

"When the brain focuses on multiple tasks, the transition time required to alternate focus can be up to a minute, so the amount of additional time required to switch mental gears can accumulate rapidly and cost a multitasker a substantial amount of extra time rather than saving them time. In essence, the multitasker looks busy, but they are actually wasting more time than someone singularly focused on one task."

Lydia Michaels, Write 10K in a Day, 2021

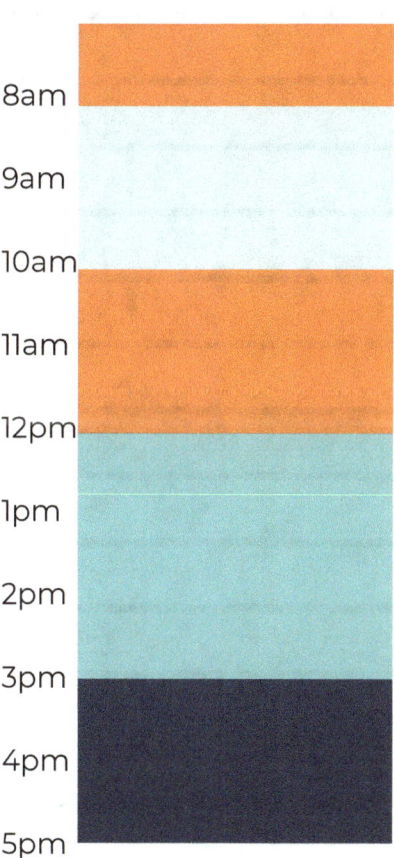

To task batch your typical day, color-code your schedule. Use specific colors that are easily differentiated for promo tasks, office maintenance, "frog tasks," and so on. By categorizing and batching, or grouping, your tasks, you will remove wasted transition time and find more time to focus on productive work.

BATCH YOUR DAY

Fill in your "typical schedule," then complete the "color key" by writing a task category into each rectangle and assigning that category a color. Batch your schedule according to the color key.

COLOR KEY

YOUR TYPICAL SCHEDULE

- 4am
- 5am
- 6am
- 7am
- 8am
- 9am
- 10am
- 11am
- 12pm
- 1pm
- 2pm
- 3pm
- 4pm
- 5pm
- 6pm
- 7pm
- 8pm
- 9pm
- 10pm
- 11pm
- 12am
- 1am
- 2am
- 3am

YOUR TASK BATCHED SCHEDULE

- 4am
- 5am
- 6am
- 7am
- 8am
- 9am
- 10am
- 11am
- 12pm
- 1pm
- 2pm
- 3pm
- 4pm
- 5pm
- 6pm
- 7pm
- 8pm
- 9pm
- 10pm
- 11pm
- 12am
- 1am
- 2am
- 3am

www.LydiaMichaelsBooks.com

WRITE 10K in a DAY

CHAPTER THIRTEEN
THE SOCIAL AUTHOR

*"When given the choice,
people will always spend their time around people they like."*

GARY VAYNERCHUK, THANK YOU ECONOMY, 2010

THE SOCIAL AUTHOR
AUTOMATE YOUR LIFE

When we automate our work, we convert the process so that it can operate automatically. By setting up automated technology in our business, we limit exposure to social media, stay relevant as a brand, save time, and increase productivity.

"Social media is one of the greatest distractions that keep authors from writing."

Lydia Michaels, Write 10K in a Day, 2

CONSISTENCY IS KEY

Brands build a following by inspiring, educating, and entertaining others. Consistently post content that viewers will return to see because it satisfies a need. Many authors use daily themes to build consistency such as "Motivational Monday" or "Tuesday Tips" or "Throw Back Thursday" and so on. Use the space below to assign a theme to each day of the week.

Use the grid below to determine monthly themes based on holidays, book anniversaries, character birthdays, special events in your life or in the life of your company, and so on.

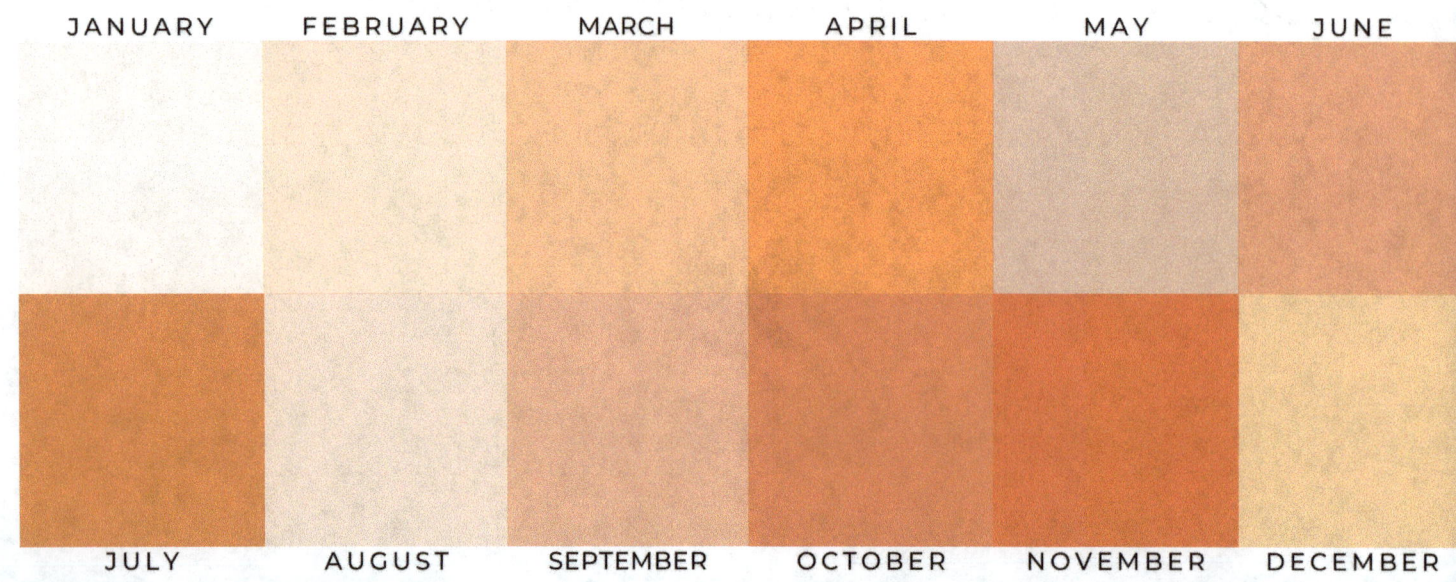

THE SOCIAL AUTHOR HASHTAGS

Use the grid below to create a quick reference of hashtags for each specific book series.

A *HASHTAG* IS A WORD OR PHRASE PRECEDED BY A HASH SIGN (#), USED ON SOCIAL MEDIA TO IDENTIFY DIGITAL CONTENT ON A SPECIFIC TOPIC.

SERIES TITLE: _____

SERIES TITLE: _____

SERIES TITLE: _____

SERIES TITLE: _____

SERIES TITLE: _____

SERIES TITLE: _____

SERIES TITLE: _____

SERIES TITLE: _____

www.LydiaMichaelsBooks.com

Chapter Fourteen
Social Monetization

"An entrepreneur with strong network makes money even when he is asleep."

AMIT KALANTRI, WEALTH OF WORDS

DISCUSSION QUESTIONS

CHAPTER FOURTEEN
SOCIAL MONETIZATION

Being a social salesperson means providing a service or product that fulfills a need or resolves a problem for the customer. Think about the messaging of your brand. What problem are you solving for the consumer? Why should they follow you? Do not focus on the sale, but rather, how you can help others. How are you helping?

YOUR ANSWER

QUESTIONS & THOUGHTS

GROUP DISCUSSION NOTES

BRAND IDENTITY

"Know your brand. Know your preferred fonts, your codes for your brand's color schemes, and your messaging. These details should be at your fingertips at all times if you want a cohesive display."

Lydia Michaels, Write 10K in a Day, 2021

BRAND FONTS:

_____
_____
_____
_____
_____

BRAND COLORS & CODES

_____
_____
_____
_____
_____

BRAND VIBE:

_____
_____
_____
_____
_____

BRAND NETWORK:

_____
_____
_____
_____
_____

WHO IS YOUR AUDIENCE

"Identify your audience and start recruiting. Interact with authors who write similar books."

Lydia Michaels, Write 10K in a Day, 2021

List the qualities of your audience according to the following:

GENDER OR SEXUAL IDENTITY:

GENRES & SUBGENRES:

AGE:

INTERESTS:

CONTENT TOPICS:

ENJOYS PHOTOS OF:

SOCIAL PLATFORMS:

WHO IS YOUR TARGET

"A good ad requires the right formula of language, imagery, and targeting to deliver the desired results."

Lydia Michaels, Write 10K in a Day, 2021

Targeting the proper audiences will help your ads.

MY DEMOGRAPHIC ACCORDING TO ANALYTICS:
_____
_____
_____
_____
_____
_____
_____
_____
_____
_____
_____
_____
_____
_____

SIMILAR BOOKS:
_____
_____
_____
_____
_____
_____

BRANDS WITH A SIMILAR VIBE:
_____
_____
_____
_____
_____
_____
_____
_____

SIMILAR AUTHORS:
_____
_____
_____
_____
_____
_____

BRANDS WITH SIMILAR MESSAGING:
_____
_____
_____
_____
_____
_____
_____
_____

CHAPTER FIFTEEN
THE PUBLISHING INDUSTRY

"*Publishing is a business. Writing may be art, but publishing, when all is said and done, comes down to dollars.*"

— NICHOLAS SPARKS, ADVICE FOR WRITERS

CONSTRUCTING QUERY LETTERS

A *QUERY LETTER* IS A FORMAL LETTER SENT TO EDITORS, LITERARY AGENTS, OR PUBLISHING HOUSES TO PROPOSE WRITING PROJECTS THAT COULD POSSIBLY LEAD TO A BOOK DEAL AND THE PUBLICATION OF ONE OR MORE MANUSCRIPTS.

SAMPLE QUERY FORMAT

Dear [full name of agent or editor],

[BOOK TITLE] **is a** [word count] **word** [genre] **novel.** [Your purpose for contact.] [If you have a referral or met the agent/editor at an event, mention that here to jog their memory.]

[The Hook or Back Cover Blurb | Often in bold and italicized]

[A brief bio including any notable credentials, such as previously published works, accolades, notable rankings, education, relevant experience, and audience, if you have an established and notable following.]

[Mention any attachments per specified guidelines. Thank you and a salutation.]

[Insert attachments]

Sincerely,
[Full Name]
[Professional email]
[Phone number]
[Website with Hyperlink]

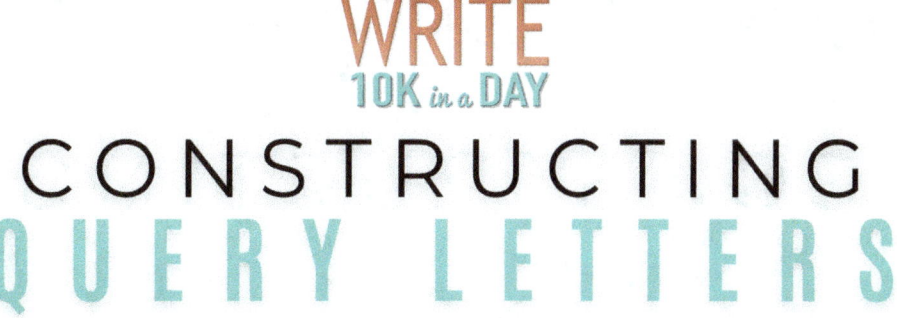
CONSTRUCTING
QUERY LETTERS

BEFORE CONSTRUCTING A QUERY LETTER, YOU SHOULD HAVE FINAL, PROOFED MANUSCRIPT AND THE FOLLOWING DETAILS:

COMPANY: _____

CONTACT PERSON: _____

BOOK TITLE: _____

WORD COUNT: _____

GENRE: _____

PROPOSAL PURPOSE: _____

REFERRAL (IF APPLICABLE): _____

BLURB:
_____
_____
_____
_____
_____
_____
_____
_____
_____
_____
_____
_____
_____

CONSTRUCTING QUERY LETTERS

BEFORE CONSTRUCTING A QUERY LETTER, YOU SHOULD HAVE FINAL, PROOFED VERSIONS OF THE FOLLOWING ELEMENTS:

NOTABLE CREDENTIALS TO INCLUDE IN BIO:

BIO (1ST PERSON):

CONSTRUCTING
QUERY LETTERS

NOW, USE THE SAMPLE FORMAT AND YOUR PERSONAL INFORMATION TO CONSTRUCT A GENERIC QUERY LETTER BELOW:

QUERY:

QUERY TRACKER

ONCE YOU BEGIN THE SUBMISSION PROCESS, IT'S WISE TO TRACK
ALL QUERIES AND RESPONSES WITH A CHART

WRITE 10K in a DAY

SAMPLE QUERY TRACKER

BOOK TITLE	COMPANY	CONTACT	DATE OF SUBMISSION	EXPIRATION DATE	METHOD OF CONTACT	ATTACHMENTS	RESPONSE

THE CRAFT
part three

Chapter Sixteen
The Creative Process

"In a sense, one can never read the book that the author originally wrote, and one can never read the same book twice."

EDMUND WILSON, THE TRIPLE THINKERS, 1976
AMERICAN AUTHOR & EDITOR FOR F. SCOTT FITZGERALD

COMMIT TO A DEADLINE

KNOWLEDGE

What areas of the industry would you like to learn more about? Set 3 education goals and challenge yourself to gain knowledge in those three areas within a measurable timeframe.

I will become more educated about:

_____ _____ _____

I commit to learning the above by: _____
DATE

PLANNING

What is your next writing project? Use the 10K methods to experiment with your creative process and accomplish your goals.

I plan to write: _____

It will have an approximate word count of _____ K.

It will be approximately _____ chapters long.

HARD WORK

I commit to working on my next novel _____ days a week for _____ hours a day. My goal is to write _____ K in a day.

CHAPTER SEVENTEEN
TRANSPORTING THE READER

> *"Readers are not sheep, and not every pen tempts them."*
>
> VLADIMIR NABOKOV, LECTURES ON LITERATURE, 1980

THE HOOK

"A good hook is the difference between a reader taking your book to the cashier or placing it back on the shelf."

Lydia Michaels, Write 10K in a Day, 2021

SET THE SCENE

CHARACTERS:

_____
_____
_____
_____
_____
_____
_____

ACTION:

_____
_____
_____
_____
_____
_____
_____

SETTING:

_____
_____
_____
_____
_____
_____
_____

THE HOOK

TASTES:

SOUNDS:

SMELLS:

SIGHTS:

PHYSICAL SENSATIONS:

EMOTIONS:

WORDS THAT **SHOW** THE EMOTIONS:

WHY DOES THE CHARACTER FEEL THIS WAY?

THE HOOK

WHAT IS THE SOURCE OF EMPATHY?

- ☐ ILLNESS
- ☐ PAIN
- ☐ FEAR
- ☐ HUMILIATION
- ☐ A SENSE OF BEING OVERWHELMED
- ☐ GRIEF
- ☐ FAILURE
- ☐ OTHER: _____

WHY SHOULD THE READER CARE?
_____
_____
_____
_____

WHY WILL THE READER ROOT FOR THE CHARACTER?
_____
_____
_____

WHAT IS CREATING A SENSE OF URGENCY?
_____
_____

WHAT IS THE SOURCE OF SUSPENSE, ANGST, WORRY, OR FEAR THAT DRIVES THE READER TO THE NEXT CHAPTER?
_____
_____

CHARACTERIZATION WEB

Set a timer for 10 minutes and brainstorm the traits of a character. Add additional bubbles as needed, expanding from general details to more specific details. Expand the web with as many details as possible.

_____
CHARACTER NAME

www.LydiaMichaelsBooks.com

CHARACTER DOSSIER

PART

USE THIS FORM TO CLARIFY THE DETAILS OF YOUR MAIN CHARACTER

NOVEL TITLE:

CHARACTER:

PHYSICAL APPEARANCE

HEIGHT:

WEIGHT:

BODY TYPE:

AGE:

SHAPE OF MOUTH:

SHAPE OF NOSE:

SHAPE OF FACE:

COLOR OF EYES:

HAIR COLOR:

HAIR TEXTURE:

HAIR LENGTH:

SKIN SHADE:

SKIN TEXTURE:

BIRTHMARKS:

SIZE OF HANDS:

CONDITION OF HANDS:

MANNER OF DRESS:

RELIGION

RELIGION:

SCHEDULE:

DEVOUT OR CASUAL:

VOICE AND SPEECH

TONE:

PITCH:

SOFT SPOKEN OR LOUD:

ACCENT:

ODD RHYTHM OF SPEECH:

NATURE OF VOCABULARY:

GRAMMATICALLY CORRECT:

MOVEMENT & GESTURES

HYPERACTIVE OR POKEY:

AWKWARD OR GRACEFUL:

EXPRESSIVE WITH HANDS:

EXPRESSIVE WITH BODY:

POSTURE:

AGILITY:

SEXUALITY

VIRGIN:

HETERO OR OTHER:

EXPERIENCE:

LIKES OR DISLIKES SEX:

GOOD OR BAD LOVER:

GUILT RIDDEN OR GUILT FREE:

FEELINGS FOR OPPOSITE SEX:

WRITE 10K in a DAY

CHARACTER DOSSIER PART 2

CATION
- TURE OF JOB:
- B PERFORMANCE:
- E OR DISLIKE THE WORK:
- -WORKERS' OPINION OF HIM/HER:
- SS'S OPINION OF HIM/HER:

ST LIFE
- O.B.:
- ACE OF BIRTH:
- RENTS' CLASS:
- THER'S OCCUPATION:
- OTHER'S OCCUPATION:
- HNICITY:
- ILDHOOD TRAUMAS:
- BLINGS:
- UCATION:
- ILDHOOD HOBBIES:
- ILDHOOD DEFEATS:
- ILDHOOD TRIUMPHS:
- B HISTORY:
- ARITAL STATUS:
- FLUENTIAL PERSON IN LIFE:
- HY THAT PERSON WAS INFLUENTIAL:

SKILLS & TALENTS
- GENERAL SKILLS:
- SPECIAL TALENTS:
- TOPIC OF WISDOM:

OTHER
- FEARS:
- DREAMS:
- PLEASURES:
- IDEALS:
- REGRETS:
- GENERAL LIKES:
- GENERAL DISLIKES:
- PLANS FOR FUTURE:
- SENSE OF HUMOR:
- POLITICS:
- LIKES CHILDREN Y/N:
- VALUES MONEY Y/N:
- BELIEVES IN LOVE Y/N:
- FEARS DEATH Y/N:
- USES LIQUOR OR DRUGS Y/N:

www.LydiaMichaelsBooks.com

GOAL MOTIVATION CONFLICT

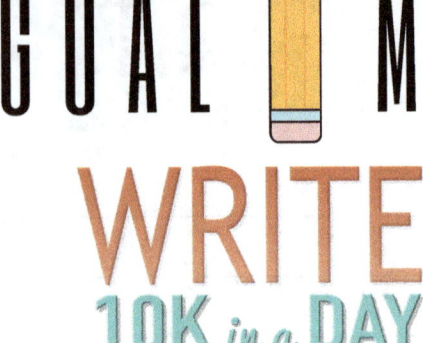

- WHAT THE CHARACTER WANTS
- WHY THE CHARACTER WANTS IT
- WHY THE CHARACTER CAN'T HAVE IT

CHARACTER NAME: _____

INTERNAL   EXTERNAL

G
M
C

CHARACTER NAME: _____

INTERNAL   EXTERNAL

G
M
C

LAYERING SUSPENSE

"With every complication, the character's situation should get darker, and the reader's angst should grow. Quality writers will connect complications, forming a secret bridge of events, where one arbitrary decision causes a seemingly unrelated obstacle down the road."

Lydia Michaels, *Write 10K in a Day*, 2021

USE THE FLOW CHART BELOW TO CONNECT EVENTS IN YOUR PLOT.

EVENT #1

- PROBLEM
- ACTION
- SOLUTION

CONSEQUENCE →

EVENT #2

- PROBLEM
- ACTION
- SOLUTION

CONSEQUENCE ↓

EVENT #3

- PROBLEM
- ACTION
- SOLUTION

CONSEQUENCE →

EVENT #4

- PROBLEM
- ACTION
- SOLUTION

PLOT WAVES

USING ONLY A FEW WORDS, FILL IN THE FIGURE BELOW TO SKETCH OUT THE ACTION SCENES OF YOUR PLOT.

"A plot is forever in motion. It is a back-and-forth pattern that swells and retreats progressively, maintaining a balanced pace."

Lydia Michaels, *Write 10K in a Day*, 2021

HOOK | LULL | ACTION | LULL | ACTION | LULL | ACTION | LULL | ACTION

DESCRIBE THE SCENE

WRITE 10K in a DAY

BOOK BIBLE

MAPPING YOUR FICTIONAL WORLD

 Maps are a key part to keeping details of a fictional world organized in a Book Bible. In the space below, draw a map of an area central to your story. It can be a city, town, home, commercial establishment, office, or anywhere your characters might gather for more than one scene.

BOOK BIBLE

TRACE YOUR CHARACTER'S FAMILY TREE

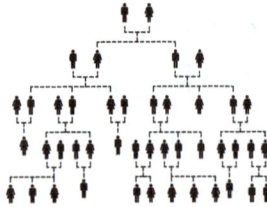

To create a family tree, trace your character's lineage back to the eldest relative mentioned in the plot and place the elder at the top branch. Use vertical lines to show offspring and horizontal lines to convey siblings or partners. Connect partners with dotted lines and use solid strokes for bloodlines. Always include full names, dates of birth, and dates of death.

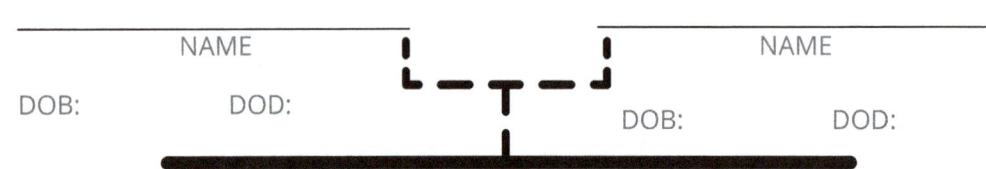

BOOK BIBLE
MAKE A GENERAL TIMELINE OF YOUR CHAPTERS.

TITLE:

TIMEFRAME:

CHAPTER:

CHAPTER:

CHAPTER:

CHAPTER:

CHAPTER:

WRITE 10K in a DAY

CHAPTER:

CHAPTER:

CHAPTER:

CHAPTER:

CHAPTER:

CHAPTER:

CHAPTER EIGHTEEN
PLOT

> "But my philosophy is that plot advancement is not what the experience of reading fiction is about. If all we care about is advancing the plot, why read novels? We can just read Cliffs Notes."
>
> — GEORGE R. R. MARTIN

GET YOUR ACTS TOGETHER

DECIDE WHICH MAJOR EVENTS BELONG IN ACT I, II, OR III OF YOUR STORY.

Act I is the setup. Build your world and characters. Establish GMCs without explicitly spelling out the GMC. Show, don't tell.

Act II begins when a choice is made. This is a fork in the road, and the protagonist sets off on an adventure. Life is about to change. Act II is layered and revealing but also unpredictable.

Act III is a major setback that causes a massive change of plans. Things about to get very uncomfortable. The third act is the most intense part of the story. Nothing is certain and it can make or break the character.

ACT I

ACT II

ACT III

The Write Fiction 10K in a Day Formula

To solve for WPC (words per chapter) divide W (the word count) by C (the number of chapters).

Formula for Words Per Chapter:
W ÷ C = WPC

Example:
60,000 words ÷ 40 chapters = 1,500 words per chapter

Based on your expectations, your novel will be _____ words. (W)

Based on your expectations, your novel will be _____ chapters. (C)

_____ ÷ _____ = _____
     W   C   WPC

WRITE 10K in a DAY OUTLINE

THIS OUTLINE IS ONLY A GUIDE

Traditional story arcs use percentages to measure plot points, but writers typically measure progress by word count.

Industry standard recognizes 60-90k words as a traditional fiction novel length.

A scene or chapter, based on this standard, will typically require 1,500 -2,250 words, but there are always exceptions.

WRITE 10K in a DAY

IN THIS SAMPLE

**WE WILL USE
A 60K WORD NOVEL**
(A Commercial Standard)

**THAT IS:
40 CHAPTERS**

1,500 WORD CHAPTERS

1% = 600 WORDS

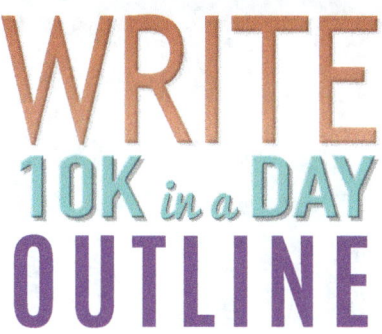

WRITE 10K in a DAY OUTLINE

01 THE HOOK

- A glimpse into the flawed world of the protagonist
- Start with ACTION!
- Showcase the character's personality and life before any personal evolution takes place
- Chapter 1 should greatly contrast with the last chapter

02 THE CONFLICT

- Presents a problem (the internal and external conflicts)
- Express the theme of the GMC: GOAL, MOTIVATION, CONFLICT but don't give away the full MOTIVATION and GOAL just yet
- Focus on explicitly summarizing the "conflict" for the reader

	INTERNAL	EXTERNAL
G	*What they want...*	*What they want...*
M	*Why they want it...*	*Why they want it...*
C	*Why they can't have it...*	*Why they can't have it...*
NEED	*Driving Passion*	*Evolved Truth*

www.LydiaMichaelsBooks.com

WRITE 10K in a DAY OUTLINE

03 THE GOAL
- Showcase the supporting characters
- Hint at the theme (the need)
- Reiterate the protagonist's GOAL from the GMC (the want)

04 THE MOTIVATION
- What is the incentive that motivates the character?
- New, life-altering information is revealed
- An event catapults the protagonist into a new world
- There is no going back to the way it was before

05 THE OPTIONS
- Protagonist debates what to do next
- Questions what the solution is
- A fork appears in the road with multiple tines
- Evaluate and discard
- Every option reveals a complication

06 THE CRUSH OF PRESSURE
- Time is running out
- No easy solution
- Tally and reject options based on complications they might cause
- The protagonist faces an unpredictable path ahead

07 THE RELUCTANCE TO CHANGE
- Protagonist hesitates because they are reluctant to change
- Reveal character traits based on the protagonist being forced into a less than favorable circumstance

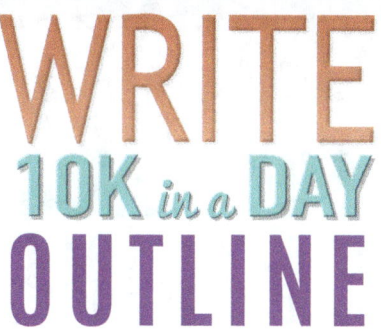
WRITE 10K in a DAY OUTLINE

08 **THE FORK**
- The protagonist has chosen a path and sets out on a new adventure
- The first step into a new world
- Reluctance lingers but the character is moving forward

A NOTABLE SHIFT

09 **THE HELPER**
- The protagonist meets a new character who will act as a guide in this new world
- The helper will ultimately help the protagonist realize the theme (the NEED) without explicitly giving it away
- The helper is devoted to helping the protagonist meet their NEEDS
- The helper will not be swayed by the character's WANTS

10 **THE ADAPTATION**
- An exciting and action-packed journey expands
- The protagonist attempts to adapt to the new world
- The protagonist is either a natural or a disaster
- An evolution begins
- Time is passing

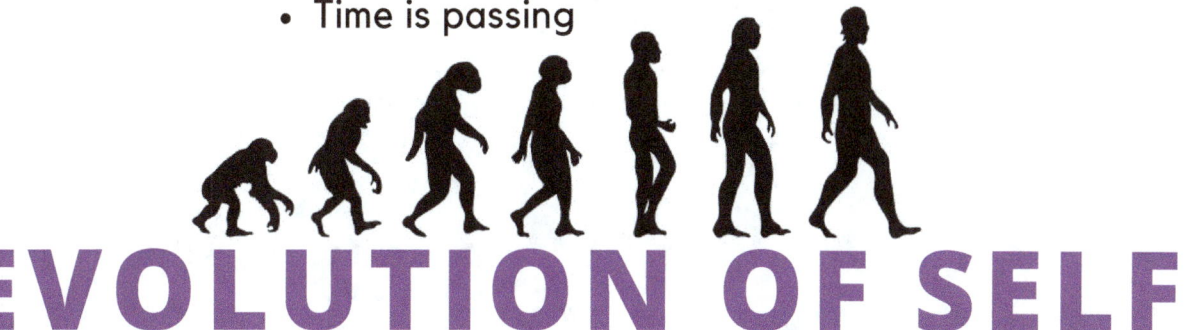

EVOLUTION OF SELF

11 — THE EFFORT

- An action chapter
- The protagonist is learning from their mistakes
- The character earns the right to triumph and the reader wants to see them succeed
- A stage of experimentation, new challenges, and a new way of life

Think Anastasia attempting to live as a submissive (Fifty Shades of Grey)

STRUGGLE VS TRIUMPH

PROTAGONIST IS EITHER A NATURAL IN THIS NEW ENVIRONMENT

Think Bella as a newborn vampire (Breaking Dawn)

OR PROTAGONIST IS A DISASTER UNDER NEW CIRCUMSTANCES

Think hockey player trying to figure skate (The Cutting Edge)

12 — THE ACCLIMATION

- Protagonist settles into a new routine
- There still remains a sense of old self and the false belief that things could possibly return to the way they were
- A hidden sense of longing

Think Elaina's search for "The Cure" after becoming a vampire (Vampire Diaries).

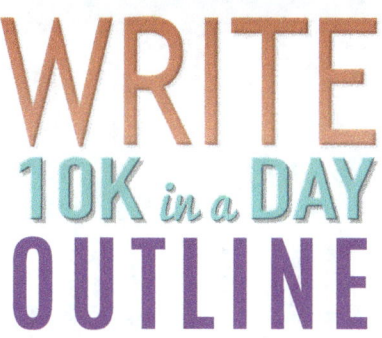

WRITE 10K in a DAY OUTLINE

13 THE PROGRESS

- What is motivating the protagonist to keep trying?
- A glimpse at the protagonist's progress
- How has the character adapted to their new circumstances (Struggle vs. Triumph)
- Time is progressing with the character
- Hints of acceptance
- Momentarily forgets how things used to be but not completely
- Settling in

Think of Belle, making the most of captivity in the Beast's castle, skating, having snowball fights, reading, and dining together... (Beauty & The Beast).

14 THE EXTERNAL SETBACK

- Revisit the protagonist's external GOALS
- External CONFLICT is revisited (is it still the same?)
- External MOTIVATION is re-examined
- Show limitations ahead and lessons learned in the past
- Possible flashback scene (Only if properly written with deep point of view)
- There is still room for growth

15 THE INTERNAL SETBACK

- Revisit the protagonist's internal GOALS
- Internal CONFLICT is revisited (is it still the same?)
- Internal MOTIVATION re-examined
- There is still reluctance to *fully* change
- WHY are things not completely working out yet?

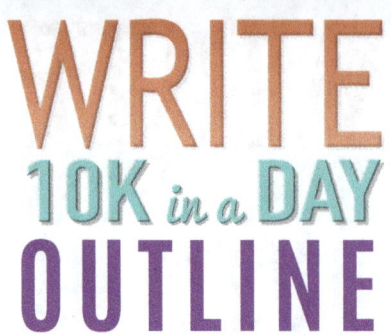

16 — THE HINT OF EVOLUTION

- A sign of growth in the protagonist's thinking
- Things are not as bad as they first seemed
- GMC shifts slightly due to the journey thus far and recent revelations

Think of the moment when Elizabeth considers Mr. Darcy might not be as uptight as he seems (Pride & Prejudice).

Also think of the moment Mark Darcy tells Bridget Jones that he likes her just the way she is (Bridget Jones' Diary).

17 — THE REALITY

- The fun stops and reality strikes hard
- The protagonist is no longer considered "new" in the new world and the "boot camp" has concluded
- Realizations occur
- The protagonist will either love or hate it

Consider Daisy Buchanan after she is finally living the life of luxury she assumed she wanted. But she's unsatisfied and wants to have an affair with Gatsby (The Great Gatsby).

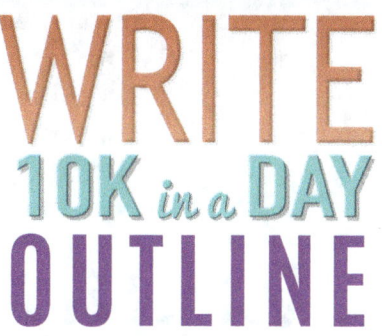

18   **THE FALSE CONCLUSION**
- A happy solution appears (but it was too easy)
- An outcome is masquerading as the conclusion
- It feels like things have wrapped up too soon
- The character has become so comfortable, they are taking the situation for granted
- Be very clear about the TRIUMPH or STRUGGLE status of the character, because things are about to flip

Consider the moment Julia Roberts finally breaks her rule and kisses Richard Gere on the mouth (Pretty Woman). This is a triumph for love and the viewer believes they will live happily ever after.

19   **THE TWIST**
- Surprise the reader with an unexpected game changer
- Shatter all illusions of security (or defeat if the protagonist has been on a losing streak)
- If the protagonist's journey has been a rise of TRIUMPH, they will suffer a tragic fall
- If the protagonist's journey has been a spiral of STRUGGLE, they will finally enjoy a massive win!
- This is the pivotal point of a dramatic shift, so prepare for turbulence ahead!
- End the chapter on a cliffhanger

WRITE 10K in a DAY OUTLINE

20 — THE PUSH

- The protagonist must declare himself or herself an irrevocable part of the new world
- Indulge in a little fanfare and make a big production of the declaration if fitting
- The character is "all in" and there's no going back
- The character surrenders to the circumstances and accepts the inevitable change
- A pivotal point
- The mid-point of the story
- Stakes are now much higher
- There is a lasting sense of urgency as if a clock is ticking and they are running out of time

Think when Katniss accepts that she is the chosen one and her loyalty shifts from self-serving to helping the people (The Hunger Games).

THE HALFWAY MARK

21 — THE POLAR SHIFT

- Past the pivotal point of a shift, the character's luck is now speeding in the opposite direction
- If the protagonist has been on a downward spiral, the failures have shifted to a massive streak of good luck and success
- If the protagonist has been on a triumphant rise, their luck has run out and things are unravelling
- This all relates the the dramatic plot shift in Chapter 19 a.k.a. THE TWIST

Think when Celie finally stands up to Mister and escapes her suppressed life with Shug Avery (The Color Purple).

OR

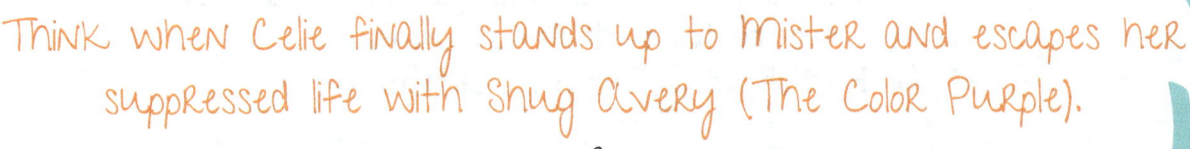

Note the changes in luck after Rose decides to leave Cal for Jack, just as the Titanic hits the iceberg (Titanic).

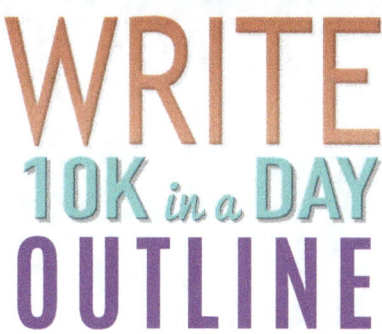

22 — THE DIFFERENCE
- Show the contrast between now and before
- Draw the reader's attention to the differences

23 — THE EXTERNAL VILLAINS
- There is a clearly defined OBSTACLE preventing the protagonist from reaching their EXTERNAL GOAL
- An external villain can be a character, a circumstance, an illness, or any obstacle otherwise known as the EXTERNAL CONFLICT
- Remind the reader that the EXTERNAL CONFLICT still exists and continues to threaten the protagonist's success

24 — THE INTERNAL VILLAINS
- INTERNAL villains are typically rooted in fear
- What did the protagonist fear most in the hook?
- Reiterate that motivating FEAR

25 — THE COMPROMISE
- The protagonist must compromise something valuable in order to move on (possibly his or her principles)
- This is a difficult choice
- This decision should create a sense of discomfort or unease in the reader, forcing the author, reader, and characters out of their comfort zones

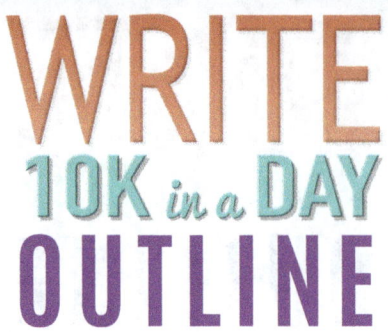

26 — THE INTERNAL CONFLICT
- The protagonist's FEAR rears its ugly head
- The protagonist is courageous but terrified
- The protagonist is halted from reaching their INTERNAL goal because they still haven't conquered their FEAR

27 — THE PROBLEM WITH NON-CONFRONTATIO[N]
- By sidestepping a problem to avoid confronting the FEAR, a new problem is introduced
- Circumstances worsen
- Shortcuts cause longer delays in the end

28 — THE CRISIS
- INTERNAL and EXTERNAL CONFLICTS collide
- The protagonist is forced into a corner
- CONFLICTS (fears and villains) grow in size and consequence
- Choices are limited due to circumstances

29 — THE ABSOLUTE WORST POSSIBLE CHOICE OF ALL
- No matter how the hero has been performing, the choice made here will cut him or her down
- Massive loss
- Something or someone should die (could be the death of privilege, freedom, a loved one, a possession, etc.)
- Leave the reader stunned and angry

30 THE FALL
- The drop off a cliff to a long fall
- Major setback
- All is lost

THE THREE-QUARTER MARK

31 THE LOWEST LOW
- The protagonist hits rock bottom
- A sense of absolute defeat
- A heartbroken hero
- Lost
- Hopeless
- The protagonist must process everything that's taken place and brought them to this point

32 THE SOLUTION
- After much reflection, the protagonist FINALLY grasps the THEME and understands what they WANTED was not what they NEEDED
- They know what they must do to resolve both INTERNAL and EXTERNAL CONFLICTS

33 THE LESSON
- Protagonist proves their understanding of the THEME in motion and dialogue
- The author spells out the THEME or LESSON to the reader

34 — THE PREPARATION

- The good guys are on the move!
- Action chapter
- Protagonist gathers all resources needed: knowledge, weapons, friends, supplies
- The protagonist is not taking any chances and will not underestimate the enemy

Consider the movie Home Alone when Kevin McCallister preps the house with endless booby traps before the Wet Bandits arrive.

35 — THE EXECUTION OF A PLAN

- The protagonist (and allies) moves forward with a plan
- Take the first steps into action but stop on the precipice of something big and unexpected
- End the chapter on a TWIST & CLIFFHANGER
- There's no way the reader can put the book down now!

36 — THE PRICE OF SACRIFICE

- The loss of security, possibly the death of a beloved side character or a breakup, has galvanized the protagonist into action and the "loss" should not be in vain.
- The loss has given the protagonist a purpose
- Action chapter
- Show the hero's resolute devotion to the cause

37 — THE PROOF

- Win or lose, the hero is committed to the very end
- The protagonist must prove their devotion and worth
- The culmination of all events have led to this very moment
- Death is no deterrent
- *Charge!!!*

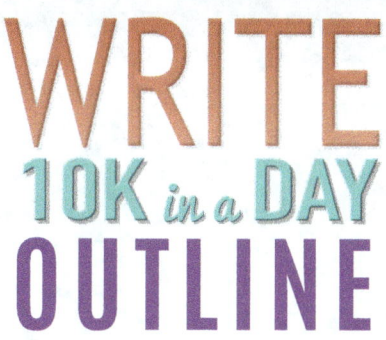

38 THE GREATEST WEAPON OF ALL
- If FEAR is the greatest obstacle, COURAGE is the greatest weapon
- This is an exquisite scene of action that should be choreographed by a chill-inducing film score performed by every instrument in a symphony to show every emotion possible
- Victory is on the line, but, win or lose, a lesson has been learned, and it was worth the cost

39 THE CLIMAX
- Get as crazy as your quill allows!
- Crank up the tension until it's unbearable!
- Build to that final blow, and then...
- VICTORY! But for who?
- The author must decide a victor
- If the villain wins, the lesson belongs to the reader
- If the hero wins, victory belongs to the characters
- In the end, either the villains or heroes are defeated

40 THE AFTERMATH
- A glimpse into the aftermath of the adventure
- This chapter will contrast with Chapter One: THE HOOK
- Show a dramatic evolution and personal growth
- So much has been learned
- It was all worth it in the end

THE END

Use the *Write 10K in a Day Outline* as a blueprint for your novel. Remember, the chapters and word count can be adapted to your needs. Simply apply the *Write 10K in a Day Formula* to your expectations and group the outlined plot points as needed to shorten the number of chapters and work within your desired word count. But try to keep events occurring in this traditional order of a linear narrative story arc. Writing a well-rounded novel is all about accomplishing certain objectives, which can be achieved at any length.

GROUP THE FOLLOWING PLOT POINTS HOWEVER YOU, THE CREATOR, SEE FIT:

1. The Hook
2. The Conflict
3. The Goal
4. The Motivation
5. The Options
6. The Crush of Pressure
7. The Reluctance to Change
8. The Fork
9. The Helper
10. The Adaptation
11. The Effort
12. The Acclimation
13. The Progress
14. The External Setback
15. The Internal Setback
16. The Hint of Evolution
17. The Reality
18. The False Conclusion
19. The Twist
20. The Push
21. The Polar Shift
22. The Difference
23. The External Villains
24. The Internal Villains
25. The Compromise
26. The Internal Conflict
27. The Problem with Non-Confrontation
28. The Crisis
29. The Absolute Worst Possible Choice of All
30. The Fall
31. The Lowest Low
32. The Solution
33. The Lesson
34. The Preparation
35. The Execution of a Plan
36. The Price of Sacrifice
37. The Proof
38. The Greatest Weapon of All
39. The Climax
40. The Aftermath

TITLE: _____ SERIES: _____

START DATE: _____ DEADLINE: _____

CHARACTER: _____

	INTERNAL	EXTERNAL
G		
M		
C		

CHARACTER: _____

	INTERNAL	EXTERNAL
G		
M		
C		

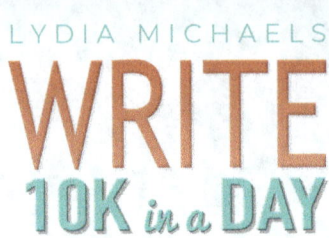

01 THE HOOK

02 THE CONFLICT

03 THE GOAL

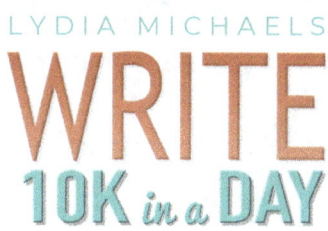

04 THE MOTIVATION

05 THE OPTIONS

06 THE CRUSH OF PRESSURE

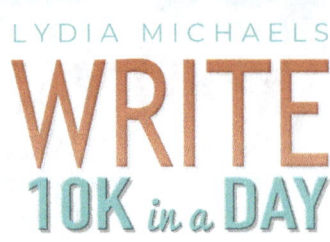

07 THE RELUCTANCE TO CHANGE

08 THE FORK

09 THE HELPER

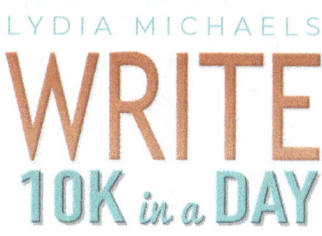

10 THE ADAPTATION

11 THE EFFORT

12 THE ACCLIMATION

13 THE PROGRESS

14 THE EXTERNAL SETBACK

15 THE INTERNAL SETBACK

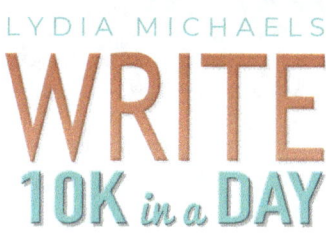

16 THE HINT OF EVOLUTION

17 THE REALITY

18 THE FALSE CONCLUSION

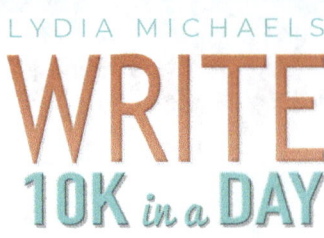

19 THE TWIST

20 THE PUSH

21 THE POLAR SHIFT

22. THE DIFFERENCE

23. THE EXTERNAL VILLAINS

24. THE INTERNAL VILLAINS

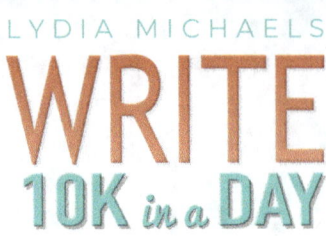

25 THE COMPROMISE

26 THE INTERNAL CONFLICT

27 THE PROBLEM WITH NON-CONFRONTATION

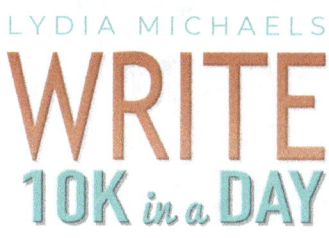

28 THE CRISIS

29 THE ABSOLUTE WORST CHOICE OF ALL

30 THE FALL

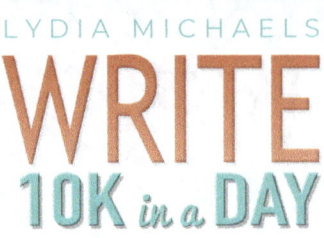

31 THE LOWEST LOW

32 THE SOLUTION

33 THE LESSON

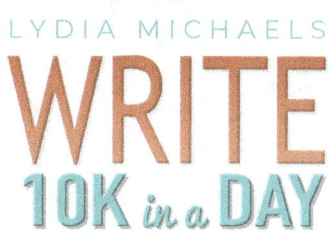

34 THE PREPARATION

35 THE EXECUTION OF A PLAN

36 THE PRICE OF SACRIFICE

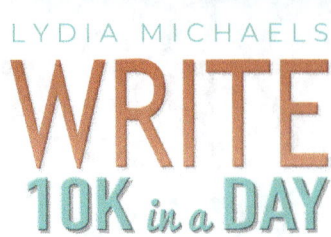

37 THE PROOF

38 THE GREATEST WEAPON OF ALL

39 THE CLIMAX

THE AFTERMATH

CHAPTER NINETEEN
THE ART OF WRITING

"*Write freely and as rapidly as possible and throw the whole thing on paper. Never correct or rewrite until the whole thing is down. Rewriting in the process is usually found to be an excuse for not going on. It interferes with flow and rhythm which can only come from a kind of unconscious association with the material.*"

JOHN STEINBECK,
NOBEL PRIZE WINNER AND AMERICAN AUTHOR OF
THE GRAPES OF WRATH AND *OF MICE AND MEN*

WRITE 10K in a DAY
REVERSE IMMERSION WRITING CHECKLIST

To better understand the various writing styles and the **Reverse Immersion Writing** approached, please visit Part Three of *Write 10K in a Day*, THE CRAFT.

- ☐ Soundtrack
- ☐ Interview with experienced professionals
- ☐ YouTube research
- ☐ Cuisine research
- ☐ Create a vision board
- ☐ Experience the language and speak to people of the culture
- ☐ Explore Google Maps
- ☐ Confuse streaming channels like Netflix with requests for movies from locations specific to the culture you're writing
- ☐ Complete a character dossier for all main characters
- ☐ Outline a story arc
- ☐ Create a cocoon of texture around your work area
- ☐ _____
- ☐ _____

www.LydiaMichaelsBooks.com

CHAPTER TWENTY
THE JOB OF EDITING

> *"Kill your darlings, kill your darlings, even when it breaks your egocentric little scribbler's heart, kill your darlings."*
>
> STEPHEN KING, ON WRITING: A MEMOIR OF THE CRAFT, 2000

WRITE 10K in a DAY
COMMON TYPOS CHECKLIST

Based on your personal history, create a list of common typos found in your manuscripts. Make a habit of scanning for such typos after you complete a first draft.

INCORRECT	CORRECT	INCORRECT	CORRECT
COMMON TYPO	SHOULD BE	COMMON TYPO	SHOULD BE

WRITE 10K in a DAY — DEEP POINT OF VIEW CHECKLIST

Remove the following words from your manuscript by replacing them with statements that take the reader deeper into the character's point of view.

- Feel
- Felt
- Hear
- Heard
- Look
- Looked
- Saw
- See
- Smell
- Smelled
- Sound
- Stared
- Taste
- Tasted
- Touch
- Touched
- Watch
- Watched

"When written exceptionally well, deep point of view disguises the mechanics of a book and establishes a trust between the reader and author where the reader is the passenger, resigned to simply enjoy the ride, without thinking about maps or traffic or if the check engine light is on."

Lydia Michaels, *Write 10K in a Day*, 2021

DISCUSSION QUESTIONS
CHAPTER TWENTY
THE JOB OF EDITING

Did you remember not to "bury the lede"? Secondary characters often drive readers to the next book in a series. Be sure to lead the reader on by dropping hints about secondary characters that create a sense of temptation. How can you lead the character to other books? What teasers can you go back and add to beef up the series arc?

YOUR ANSWER

QUESTIONS & THOUGHTS

GROUP DISCUSSION NOTES

Chapter Twenty-One: The Takeaway

> "When I was a little girl, I won a gold medal for figure skating, not because I was the best competitor on the ice that day, but because I fell in the middle of my routine and immediately got up and tried again. We never truly fail as long as we continue to rise. Rising, again and again, is the only way to reach the satisfying end."
>
> — LYDIA MICHAELS, WRITE 10K IN A DAY, 2021

DISCUSSION QUESTIONS

CHAPTER TWENTY-ONE
THE TAKEAWAY

After reviewing the Write 10K in a Day methods, do you feel in more control of your creative process and success? What practices do you feel will help you most?

YOUR ANSWER

QUESTIONS & THOUGHTS

GROUP DISCUSSION NOTES

DISCUSSION QUESTIONS

CHAPTER TWENTY-ONE
THE TAKEAWAY

Are there parts of the Write 10K in a Day methods that you would like to revisit? Are there areas that you found confusing? Where would you request more information be added to the series? Have you considered emailing Lydia Michaels at Lydia@LydiaMichaelsBooks.com or reaching out to her on Instagram @Write10KinaDay? She would love to hear from you!

YOUR ANSWER

QUESTIONS & THOUGHTS

GROUP DISCUSSION NOTES

DISCUSSION QUESTIONS
CHAPTER TWENTY-ONE
THE TAKEAWAY

Successful authors have a strong network of peers. Who do you know that would benefit from some or all of the strategies taught in the Write 10K in a Day series? Create a list of authors and writers you will contact to recommend Write 10K in a Day and possibly join your mastermind group.

YOUR ANSWER

QUESTIONS & THOUGHTS

GROUP DISCUSSION NOTES

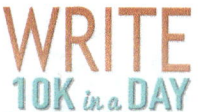

GET THE FULL EXPERIENCE!

The **Write 10K in a Day Workbook** is part of the *Write 10K in a Day* series which includes Lydia Michaels's groundbreaking author guide, **Write 10K in a Day: Avoid Burnout and Unleash Your Prolific Potential** (available in print, digital, and **audiobook**) and the **Write 10K in a Day Author Planner**.

To fully understand the concepts taught in the **Write 10K in a Day** series, authors are encouraged to read the complete collection, utilizing the accompaniment texts that apply the theories examined. Once strategies are adapted to fit an author's individual creative process, chances of burnout will diminish and productivity will increase. With practice, writers can reach goals of writing 10K in a day while living a balanced life.

For a more comprehensive look at business essentials, such as the publishing process, managing social media, finding a healthy balance between life and time on the job, and achieving sustainable success in the book industry, read *Write 10K in a Day*--the book that started it all. Michaels shares years of experience in a warm and personal manner that grips the reader, inspires, and even gets a few laughs.

For educational videos, author resources, and ongoing inspiration, follow Lydia Michaels and the *Write 10K in a Day* series on Instagram **@Write10KinaDay** and **@Lydia_Michaels_Books**.

Do you have suggestions to improve this workbook or other books in the Write 10K in a Day series?

Email Lydia Michaels at Lydia@LydiaMichaelsBooks.com.

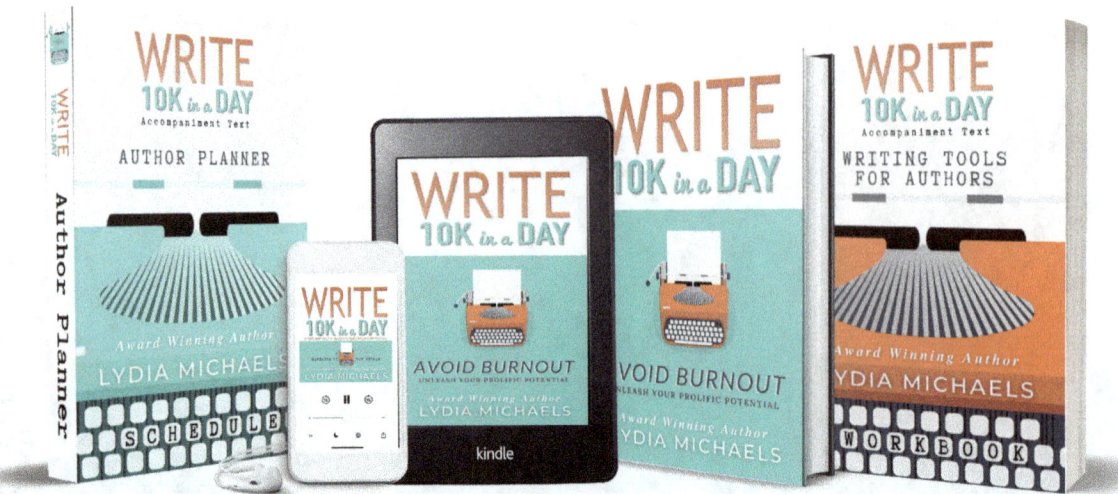

ABOUT THE AUTHOR

Lydia Michaels is the author of over forty novels and the consecutive winner of the *2018 & 2019 Author of the Year Award* from *Happenings Media*, as well as the recipient of the *2014 Best Author Award* from the *Courier Times*. She has been featured in *USA Today*, *Romantic Times Magazine*, *Love & Lace*, and more. As the host and founder of the *East Coast Author Convention*, the *Behind the Keys Author Retreat*, and *Read Between the Wines*, she continues to celebrate her growing love for romance novels and her readers around the world.

Lydia is happily married to her childhood sweetheart. Some of her favorite things include the scent of paperback books, listening to her husband play piano, escaping to her coastal home at the Jersey Shore, cheap wine, 80's pop culture, coffee, and kilts. She hopes to meet you soon at one of her many upcoming events.

Please follow and/or reach out to Lydia Michaels through email or social media. She is most interactive with bloggers, authors, and fans on the following platforms:

Email:
Lydia@LydiaMichaelsBooks.com

Instagram:
@Lydia_Michaels_Books
www.instagram.com/lydia_michaels_books

Facebook:
www.Facebook.com/LydiaMichaels

TikTok:
@lydiamichaels
www.tiktok.com/@lydiamichaels

BOOKS BY LYDIA MICHAELS

Write 10K in a Day: Avoid Burnout and Unleash Your Prolific Potential
Write 10K in a Day Workbook
Write 10K in a Day Author Planner
Wake My Heart
The Best Man
Love Me Nots
Pining For You
Original Sin
Dark Exodus
Sugar
Hurt
Calamity Rayne: Gets a Life
Calamity Rayne: Back Again
Forfeit
Lost Together
Atonement
Almost Priest
Beautiful Distraction
Irish Rogue
British Professor
Broken Man
Controlled Chaos
Intentional Risk
Hard Fix
First Comes Love
If I Fall
Something Borrowed
Falling In
Breaking Out
Coming Home
Sacrifice of the Pawn
Queen of the Knight
Breaking Perfect
Protege
Blind
Untied
La Vie en Rose
Simple Man
Remember Me

NOTES

NOTES

NOTES

NOTES